On the Seventh Day of April... Superman Died

The Justin Whitaker Story

By

Bob Lanciault

PublishAmerica
Baltimore

© 2009 by Bob Lanciault.
All rights reserved. No part of this book may be reproduced, stored in a retrieval system or transmitted in any form or by any means without the prior written permission of the publishers, except by a reviewer who may quote brief passages in a review to be printed in a newspaper, magazine or journal.

First printing

PublishAmerica has allowed this work to remain exactly as the author intended, verbatim, without editorial input.

ISBN: 978-1-61546-641-2
PUBLISHED BY PUBLISHAMERICA, LLLP
www.publishamerica.com
Baltimore

Printed in the United States of America

"If I say why me, then I am wishing it (cancer) on someone else. If someone has to have it, then let that someone be me."

Justin Whitaker

As Justin Says Goodbye

On a cool September day, you were born and brought to us here.
We were gifted by your presence, as we watched you grow.
Your family and friends, touched by your spirit and energy,
Knew that in some small way, your being affected all of them.
Your beloved game of baseball allowed you to focus on the future.
Regardless of the hurdles, you stood tall to the very end.
So fragile this life can be, at a time when you seek to turn corners.
Your candle had yet to burn its full length, you hid your pains.
Afflictions of the body were ones that never affected your soul.
You vowed to fight this dreadful disease, as an athlete always does.
With sword in hand, you dared this beast and wished it into submission.
Yet the attack was relentless, and you grew tired and weak.
With a loving family, a fiancé, and lifelong friends beside you,
You suddenly knew that as you lay still and silent, you were not alone.
Number seven still held that swagger that all could clearly see.
For close to two years, this battle raged on, and never did you waver.
Amazed by the support of a loving, caring community who gave its all,
There simply was a point when you knew it was time to say goodbye.
As you lay motionless in your bed in those waning days, people visited.
Some say that you were not able to hear, yet you heard each voice.
Your spirit traveled to the Wolverine's den and beyond…you were there.
Your number seven was worn in support of your fight…you saw them.
You rose above the candlelight vigil and thanked all…you rested now.
And on a sullen April day, you died, and found your place in heaven.
As Superman flew high above the clouds, so shall you Justin Whitaker.
Never will that image fade, nor will your life here ever be forgotten.

Leaving Behind His Legacy

Justin Lee Whitaker, was born on the seventh day of September, and left us in life at the tender age of eighteen on the seventh day of April. His one year, and nine month bout with non-Hodgkin's T-Cell Lymphoma had now ended, and the valiant number seven was laid to rest. The significance of the 7th on a calendar, moved far beyond Justin's birth date, and that of his death. For years through youth baseball, and marching toward his playing days at North Stafford High School in Virginia, he proudly wore the number seven in adulation of his boyhood hero, Mickey Mantle, from the famed New York Yankees. Ironically, Mickey Mantle also aligned with the month of April, for in that same month in 1951 he broke into professional baseball. Until speaking to Justin's father Craig, I was never aware of how spiritually touching it was, when pausing to reflect on what a simple number meant to so such a kind, courageous, loving boy. As word of Justin's passing spread throughout Stafford County, Virginia, everyone had to accept the somber fact that Justin was now truly *gone*. This sad seventh day of April, marked a tragic end to the life of Justin Whitaker. The brave North Stafford teen, given the moniker of *'Superman'* because of his strength, and endless battles through adverse times, was a gift to all he touched. We cherish the number seven in a far different way now, for it is one that remains emblazoned within our hearts, reminding us daily of the fragility of life.

Tragically for Justin, the T-Cell cancer he suffered from, only accounts for roughly 1% of all lymphomas. Justin had great difficulty breathing at times, and he had predominant swelling throughout his extremities, and facial areas. Another unfortunate aspect of the T-Cell lymphoma, is that it is extremely fast growing, and once it spreads to the bone marrow, only about 40%-50% of patients can be cured. Justin held no luck in that regard either, as this insidious disease ravaged his entire body.

Justin's correlation to *Superman* arose numerous times, and often involved humorous stories, with Justin usually playing the role of a hospital court jester. On one occasion, Dr. Marcie Weil from Inova Fairfax Hospital, sought to extract bone marrow from Justin during a biopsy, and remarked that Justin's bones were extremely strong, and that it was difficult to get deep enough to attain a proper sample. In typical J.W. fashion, he simply responded by saying, *"I'm a man of steel."* It should also be noted that Justin was wearing red, and blue Superman boxers at the time. From that point on, Justin Whitaker *was* Superman. In a humorous way, future bone marrow biopsies at Inova were always referred to as *'Superman Tests.'* Once word got out about Justin's rightfully deserved nickname, the Christopher Reeve Foundation, along with many other generous souls, sent Justin a variety of Superman paraphernalia. Justin's family continued to be amazed at every turn regarding the heartfelt warmth, and support they received from everyone, especially total strangers from across the country, and across great oceans.

Superman made his presence known to other children suffering from cancer, and serious illnesses in the hospital ICU ward that housed twenty separate rooms. Justin's father Craig proudly said, that Justin always seemed to have a way about him that made all of the nurses smile. It was that little something extra within his personality that seemingly took the edge off their chaotic, daily lives dealing with so many tragic cases. Justin would stroll down the hall of the ICU and according to him, he was *"making his rounds"* as he visited with sick children who were only five or six years old at the time. Even then, Justin agonized over the terrible illnesses that implanted themselves within these small, innocent children.

Justin *did* have that smirk, a cat who ate the canary expression, one of bashfulness at times, and that I suppose, of your typically wired teenager. I remember speaking to other coaches on our teams after watching Justin standing in the batter's box.

With his bat held high, feverishly waggling it in his hands, it appeared at times that with his grip, he was attempting to squeeze water from it. He would glare out at the pitcher's mound, akin to an "I dare you" moment, and maintain this wildly animated motion with body, and bat the entire time. If he swung and missed a pitch, you would think that he had no strikes left in the count at all. He could never be labeled as that fluid, poised swinger who when finishing a cut, stood in statuesque fashion as if posing. Justin was your hands clenched, grip and rip type, seeking to drive the ball at any cost. There was one mission, and that was to sting the baseball and scamper around the bases. He was a *fighter* from the very first time I saw him at the plate, to the last moment I saw him in his room at the Inova Fairfax Hospital ICU, digging in for every minute he had left on this earth. Justin stared at the prospect of facing death, in the same way that he glared at opposing pitchers. There was no alternative *ever* but to fight in either battle, just as there was never a grey area in the way he was remembered by everyone he touched, before, and after his passing. If he was to leave life, and those that he loved so very much, it would be done *going down swinging*. That to me, was forever the true essence of Justin Whitaker.

There was one little girl, Lisa Linares, who was in the unit as well suffering from cancer. Craig remembered the first time Justin saw her in the ward. Justin was lying in bed, and before he even knew her name, Lisa peeked around the corner of Justin's door and meekly waved. She did not say a word and Justin just waved back. A short time after that, Lisa met with Justin and gave him what she called her *"favorite Barbie doll"* to comfort him. Justin put it up on a shelf, and in a quiet exchange, he offered Lisa one of his many teddy bears that were sent to him. It was during this first hello in the ICU that Justin and Lisa became friends. Lisa at the present time, is in remission with her illness.

I came to know Justin and his family well at the beginning of those awkward, formative years of teen land, while serving as a parent, and an assistant coach for several Stafford League Baseball, and area AAU baseball teams. These are the years when kids are groping with their identities, while equally battling through times when motor skills, and coordination athletically, are often not quite in fluid synchronization. I may be repeating many a person that spoke of Justin's demeanor and spirit, even during horrific times when his young body was wracked in pain, yet I must concur with everyone's assessments of Justin on all accounts.

Justin's hero, Mickey Mantle, was by far one of the most amazing baseball players of all time. In Major League Baseball today, tragic stories of steroid use splash across the headlines in reckless fashion. Those seeking fame choose to cheat themselves and the game that is cherished by so many. Not Mickey Mantle. He crushed 536 homeruns, played in 20 all star games, and won 3 MVP crowns. Justin Whitaker chose to cherish a true American hero, and he held pride when wearing his number seven in emulation of all that Mickey Mantle stood for. Mickey Mantle once said, *"it was all I lived for…to play baseball."* Anyone who knew and felt Justin's penchant for baseball, could easily attribute that same quote to him. On a plaque at Yankee Stadium, the name of Mickey Mantle stands out above all others. There are simple words etched into granite, that captured the true essence of what he stood for. It says, *"he left a legacy of unequalled courage."* Justin Lee Whitaker left us that same legacy.

Moving forward in time, during the memorial service for Justin at North Stafford High School, a packed gymnasium watched in silence as a tiny little girl was seen slowly getting out of her chair, and moving toward Justin's casket. Very few people even knew at the time who she was. A hushed crowd watched as this miniscule lady carried a single rose, raised up on her toes, and rested the flower on top of Justin's place of rest. As she had once said hello to Justin Whitaker with a wave of her hand over a year and half ago, Lisa now had the chance to say goodbye in her own private, special way. It was a child's way of telling Justin she loved him. In her heart, Lisa knew the pain inside Justin's body was gone, and in his faith, he had found eternal peace.

"A Dream Is a Wish"

I cannot possibly describe the pain and anguish within the North Stafford High School gymnasium, on the day of Justin's memorial service. It began with a somber slide show entitled, *'Justin's Journey,'* that touched on his joys and triumphs in baseball, to some of the more cherished moments in this young man's life. I watched slide after slide, and found myself pent up in pain, as flashes of Justin's AAU baseball years, cascading into a packed gymnasium, were displayed for all those in attendance. As a picture of Justin popped onto the screen in his AAU uniform, I suddenly felt like all of the air had been sucked out of my lungs. I am not ashamed to say that I audibly gasped, instantly tearing up, because the reality had finally sunk in that Justin was truly *gone*. A close friend of mine, Amy Kittell, who was an AAU parent and equally pained by his loss, fully understood the gravity of the moment. It was painfully shocking to stare at number seven on the screen. It was not a bad dream anymore. As you glanced at these moving, incredibly sad pictures of Justin's world before you, your attention riveted back to his casket front and center, and it agonizingly slapped everyone in attendance back to reality. Justin Whitaker had left us.

This Wolverine gym was no longer a place where rivals met, and sparred until the other succumbed to defeat. All you had to do was let your eyes wander, and you viewed entire *enemy* teams from Stafford County paying tribute to a man their same age, who had lost his life. It mattered not what school you played for, or whether or not you were deemed to be one of North Stafford's fiercest rivals on this day. There were no opponents present, for on this day everyone seemingly bonded in unspeakable grief. The number seven was honored on every sports uniform worn by North Stafford High School team members. Other Commonwealth District sports teams also held special tributes to Justin, adorning their uniforms and warm up shirts with his initials, and of course, his beloved number seven. Throughout an entire county and beyond, remembrances of Justin Whitaker were literally everywhere.

Justin's memorial service began with the song, *'I Can Only Imagine,'* which again unleashed a wave of sorrowful, emotional outbursts from most in attendance. Yet, the most painful song had yet to be heard on this day. When the North Stafford High School Jazzie Ladies stepped up to their respective microphones, you could sense that long before the song, *'A Dream is a Wish'* was to be sung, nine young ladies were clearly in agony. They valiantly sang painful verses, and finally as they hit the line of *'no matter how your heart is grieving,'* the floodgates erupted as most of the girls audibly sobbed and cried, as their tune turned agonizingly mournful at the finale. Without a doubt, that one line epitomized the immense grief that had penetrated each and every person in the crowded North Stafford gymnasium.

Even as the end of his life neared, and decisions were made by family members to remove Justin from life support, it was as if he truly had one swing left in him. Doctors at Inova Fairfax Hospital, explained to family members that normally, a person's heartbeat would cease to exist within fifteen to twenty minutes after removal from life support. *Superman* had another idea on this seventh day in April. Similar to many other instances when this young man battled through painful adversities and downfalls, it was as if Justin had one more thing to say about taking his last breath.

This deadly, relentless lymphoma, a horrific enemy that left Justin in severe pain and unable to walk at times, was not about to take him down now…not quite yet! If this machine was to be shut down, it was as if Justin's spirit reared up again, in an effort to wage war on this illness for just a little longer…*on his terms*. Reminiscent to a recurrence of his cancer last fall, and subsequent bone marrow transplant, *Superman* was his typical, effervescent self. Without concern for himself *ever*, Justin continued to offer us all lesson after lesson. At that point in his life, Justin, in a matter of fact tone after his bone marrow procedure soundly said, *"I will never give up."* He proved just that as his heart motored on for close to four hours after his life sustaining machine was shut down. His drive to live, and his stamina to fight a deadly enemy amazed medical professionals, loving family members, and cherished friends who stood

ON THE SEVENTH DAY OF APRIL...SUPERMAN DIED

by his side until the very end in his lonely ICU room. Justin's father Craig told me later how with each hour's passing after life support was stopped, it was abundantly clear that his son *was* a super hero. Like most who knew Justin, this was the way number seven always treated things, by digging his spikes in, and *never* giving up.

After Justin's death, Craig Whitaker forlornly recalled the sad day of April 2, 2008, at about 1:30 a.m., when Justin began experiencing seizures, and developed a fever of 103. Because he had made so many monumental strides in his arduous battle, there were few who could even fathom that in five short days, Justin would be leaving us forever. As his condition worsened, Craig knew that Justin was in great pain, and his communication skills were weakening. He could only mumble and was unable to talk in complete sentences. A 911 call was made and Justin was readied for transport to Mary Washington Hospital in Fredericksburg, VA. Justin floated in and out of consciousness, and while being attended to by medical personnel, he said, *"Dad I almost made it. I almost hit a homerun. It was a little bit short of the warning track."* Craig, in both a state of shock and immense despair, simply told Justin, *"no son, you hit one out of the park. You hit a grand slam."* Doctors would later determine that Justin's brain was swelling, yet again, he felt the need to reassure his father that he would be o.k. He would later be transported to the ICU at Inova Fairfax, where he remained until his death five days later. Justin never verbally responded to his father again. Yet, as he was being wheeled from his house to the waiting ambulance, in the fashion of a fierce, competitive athlete, he gave his dad a final, resounding, double thumbs-up gesture. This majestic thumbs-up to his dad, signified that Justin had hit a colossal grand slam, that to this day continues to rocket through the sky. You *did* hit that homerun *Superman*...a towering blast that nobody will ever soon forget.

When I met with Craig Whitaker and discussed the entire staff at Inova Fairfax, he became visibly upset and spoke of Dr. Marcie Weil and all of the nurses in nothing but be highest of terms. Craig painfully talked about the decision to remove Justin from life support, and how pained Dr. Weil was regarding the optimal point to do so. Marcie was well aware of all those around her, as well as throughout Stafford County, that were grieving about Justin's medical condition. In the end, the final weekend was left for family members and close friends to pay their last respects to Justin in the ICU. Craig had tears in his eyes as he recalled Marcie's own pains in making the decision on Monday to remove Justin from life support. The entire ICU staff grieved over a special young man who clearly impacted their lives, even while dealing with cancer patients on a daily basis. Not enough is said about those that give their lives to the medical profession. Never can there be enough thanks bestowed upon them, according to Craig. As Craig wiped tears from his eyes, he paused in silence and told me that he had just remembered something else. He had an image come back to him as we sat there talking, of a night at the house when he and Justin were relaxing watching television. It was clear, according to Craig, that Justin was very bothered about the fact that things were not looking good as it related to his declining health. Justin turned toward his father and said, *"Dad, Superman is not supposed to die right?"* Because it was so out of the blue, Craig said it stunned him and he recalled telling Justin that *"even Superman couldn't hide from kryptonite. If I find any I'll keep it away from you."* He partially laughed recalling that conversation with his son, but the tears welling in his eyes told a far different story as it related to the immense pain within his heart.

The entire Whitaker family, and those who stood by Justin's side throughout his one year and nine month ordeal, wanted to extend heartfelt thanks to artist Josie Vincent. Craig spoke to Josie relative to Justin's death and upcoming memorial service. Within two days, and without hesitation, Josie professionally made a sketch of Justin as he stood in his majestic Superman. The beautiful sketch honoring Justin and his life, was present at his viewing, as well as his memorial service. Josie Vincent never knew Justin, and gave from the heart in dedication of those who grieved. She offered a lasting image of Superman, who held the power to touch all of us.

A Mother's Unyielding Faith

"He Was Never Alone"
by Kathryn James......

I'm so sorry son...
I didn't get to hold your hand in mine...
To kiss your face my precious...
I wasn't given the time...
The doctor said you wouldn't hear...
I whispered anyway...
You're tired now my darling...
Go now...you mustn't stay...
As angels gathered round you...
I felt the whisper of their wings...
And as they spirited you away...
I thought of so many things...
"Why God why...my precious son...
Why not me instead?"
That's not the way it's supposed to be...
He just cannot be dead...
Can't the angels wait awhile?
Give me a little more time?
There's so much more I need to say...
Before I say goodbye...
Please...say you'll grant me one more hour...
I have so much to do...
Kiss and hug, and hold him close...
Before I give him to you...
Alright Lord...I trust you...
I just have to ask you see...

> Just one more little favor Lord...
> Please tell him goodbye for me.

(Kathryn James wrote this to her 'Matty' on 4/23/2000 at 3:00 a.m.)
(His mission here was finished. Our father called him home. I gave birth to an angel."
*Written in loving memory of Matthew G. Darshay
(4/24/77-8/12/95)*

    The amazing poem written above by Kathryn James, was yet another spiritualistic gift entrusted to me. I had just completed my first talk with Shelia Whitaker, Justin's mother, and was profoundly touched by her strength and faith. Shelia and I met for over two hours, yet because our conversation was so moving and emotional at times, it seemed as if only a short time had passed. After I returned to my trusty computer to take my scrawled words, and transform them into proper English, I felt the urge to search for a poignant writing, or poem that somehow aligned with the thoughts Shelia and I had shared. I came upon this beautiful, yet tragic writing by Kathryn James, who painted a moving picture of her son Matthew, and of her committed faith, that seemingly sustained her after losing him. Matthew, like Justin, passed away at the age of eighteen. As you will understand while reading of Shelia's feelings, the words written by Kathryn above, held uncanny ties to everything Shelia and I discussed during our first conversation. I was stunned as the poem ended, and Kathryn wrote of Matthew being *"called home"* by the Lord. Shelia and I talked about Justin's *"coming home"* at length, and her faith was equally as astounding as Kathryn's.

    As I returned to work the following Monday, there was an email waiting for me from Kathryn James. After I read the beautiful poem she had written, I knew that it would be a fitting tribute to Justin, while serving as a memorial to Matthew Darshay. There was a link on Matthew's memorial page that allowed me to send a note to Kathryn, asking for permission to use her poem in the book. Kathryn was honored to be contacted, and overwhelmingly gave me permission to use her words. With Kathryn, I had discussed the similar threads between what she wrote, and the manner in which Justin's mom Shelia, had reflected on her own loss.

At the close of her note, Kathryn related to me that like myself, she too had lost her parents at a very young age. In addition to that, she again stunned me by saying that other tragedies occurred in her life as well. Kathryn went on to explain that in her past, in one night, she lost her mother, and five other siblings. Kathryn's mother died at home from a cerebral hemorrhage at the age of forty two. Kathryn was only eight years old at the time. Because Kathryn's mother cared for all her children alone, the entire family was split apart, and sent to live in different places. She would later find out that one of her sisters had committed suicide in 1980, leaving two younger brothers, and one older sister unaccounted for since her mom's death in 1960. In a warm side to such loss, Kathryn said that as a result of her poem, which has been read and touched countless others worldwide, a long lost sister was found in November of 2007. They became family again as Kathryn's sister realized *who* the writer was on the other end of a computer connection. Kathryn vowed that her search for her missing brothers and sister would continue, in hope that a forty eight year gap in time could be laid to rest forever. I came away yet another time, touched by the warm heart of a stranger. These spiritual surges have now happened so many times since I began this endeavor, that frankly I have lost count.

Returning to the Whitaker family, I first met Shelia and Craig when my son Nick played AAU baseball in the Stafford, Virginia area. Nick played with the Sabres, and Justin for the Hurricanes. They were all of nine and ten years old, and literally just coming into their own as athletes. Nick would later play with Justin on the Hurricane squad as well, then they both ricocheted as teammates on the Virginia Thunder squad, where I assisted as a coach. Long story short, you got to know all the parents on most of the teams, and road trip after road trip, you learned about 'who' your players *really* were as people. Nick, Justin, and all the boys were precocious teens sowing their oats, and the great times we shared over many seasons were priceless.

I had not seen Shelia since the memorial service for Justin, and I was anxious to talk of so many things that truly, only a mother can attest to.

We sat down and began to lightly chat, and it did not escape either of us that Justin would have turned nineteen on September 7, 2008, merely three days prior. It was now five months since Justin had passed away, yet as we talked, there was an overall atmosphere of peace and serenity within the room. I felt this instant warmth in those first ten to fifteen minutes, as well as a spiritual assurance of sorts, that Justin was in good hands now. There was little question that Justin had learned a great deal of his spiritual faith from his mother.

As the lives of Shelia Whitaker, and Kathryn James seemingly intersected, before words were ever spoken between Shelia and I, you could sense a mother's loving affection for her child. In one of Kathryn's notes, she told me of days weaving into one another, and how when passing in front of a mirror, she could no longer recognize the person in the reflection. The look in Shelia's eyes reflected that same sense of loss. There were times of unfathomable fatigue, inabilities in making routine decisions, and unquestionable grief. Justin's father Craig had mentioned to me numerous times of an expectation in rounding a corner, and seeing Justin standing there smiling. Kathryn and Shelia felt those same emotions. Losing a child held larger than life ramifications in every facet of their lives. There were endless wishes in freezing time, and without question, Kathryn said it best when she added that, *"I mourned the past, survived the present, and now dreaded the future."* The loss of a child, echoed through the tear filled eyes of a parent, forced to face new days ahead far more broken and challenged than ever. Kathryn reflected on her *"forgotten faith"* that pushed her through the most difficult of times, and Shelia consistently spoke of a faith unbroken, one that *knew* Justin was safe and happy now. There is little question that for Kathryn and Shelia, along with everyone else experiencing such loss, there will forever be an inescapable emptiness. Yet, both of these strong women equally spoke of Matty and Justin on safer ground now, feeling spiritually closer to them in ways that quite frankly, only a mother could understand.

I think most would agree, that a mother's place in a child's world, is different than that of a father. It does not discredit the importance of dad within the home, but whether your child is male or female, a mother's heart and mannerisms, naturally seems to foster more open lines of communication. I remain extremely close to my two children, Nick and Alyssa, and honestly feel no discomfort in saying that their mother Sheila, is often the first to have private conversations, and ease the sporadic aches and pains of their hearts. My thoughts still drift back to my own mother who passed away when I was in my early 20's. She was the commander of the ship in my family of eight kids, who had to pull everything together after my father died. I was only fourteen when I awoke to the sounds of my father in extreme pain, as he experienced a heart attack in the living room of our home. I watched with my younger brother Steve as the ambulance pulled away, taking my father to the hospital. Tragically, he never came home. I suppose my experiences dealing with family tragedies, and my work within law enforcement for a lifetime, well suited me to be empathetic for others at the worst of times. I forever reflect on the role my mother held as we were all growing up, and the influence she had on my life. In Shelia Whitaker, I felt those same emotions, and realized in minutes how she shaped not only Justin's life, but the lives of all her children.

In my mind, I knew I wanted to get a picture of Justin from that same *'mother's perspective,'* as she watched Justin grow from a small child, to the strong man of character that he evolved into. There is little question that Craig too, as the father, had similar gifts he passed down to Justin, yet right here and now, I sought to learn of the pains of a mother losing her child. Shelia softly said that, *"I suppose I was the spiritual leader in the family. After our divorce, I would always pick Justin and Jordie up and take them to church. Jordie was four, and Justin was five at the time. Focusing on Justin, I knew right away that his faith was very strong. There was one funny time, but eerie too, when my car broke down. Justin and Jordie were in the car, and Justin said to Jordie, "let's pray." Justin put his hands on the wheel and then told me to try and start the car. Who knows why but that car turned over, and I never forgot that. I cannot describe it fully, but Justin's faith was absolutely phenomenal."*

Shelia went on to talk about Justin's youthful times. She smiled and laughed when I asked about baseball, and things that he and Jordie would do. Shelia said, *"one time, I think Justin was about seven years old and he, Jordie, and Craig were in the backyard playing with a waffle ball and bat. It was Justin's turn to bat, and Craig was pitching. Craig threw a pitch and Justin swung hard,* drilling a line drive right off of Craig's forehead. The hit shocked him I think because he fell over backwards. We all laughed later, but Justin hit that ball hard. He loved the game of baseball. One other time he and Jordie were outside, and surprised me by bringing in some dandelions. They said, "here momma," and blew a few petals off, as if to make a wish for me. They always did such sweet things."

We talked about Justin's demeanor as a child, and Shelia said that he was always such an inquisitive soul, loving to help out in the kitchen, and learn about whatever she was doing. Shelia remarked, *"he loved to help me in the kitchen when I cooked, especially when I baked cookies. But even when he was really young, Justin's eyes were always so expressive. If he wasn't feeling well, I could see it in his eyes long before he told me. That never changed. He seemed to have strep throat a lot when he was growing up, and when he got sick after the cancer, I remember thinking about how often he had strep."*

As Justin's adolescent years moved on, Shelia and I talked about what he enjoyed the most, and of his loves…dreams. Shelia said, *"Justin always loved watching police shows, and anything that was action packed. He would always talk about serving his country in the military, and of course, one day playing professional baseball. In the last year of his life, he talked a lot about joining the FBI too, and you saw that gleam in his eye. There was one day that I remember well. He said to me, "momma, what if I don't make it in baseball?" I knew that his illness was weighing on him and his mind was full of questions. All I could manage to say was, Justin, you can do anything you set your mind to. He just had that way about him that was so driven and strong."*

As our conversation moved on, Shelia talked about how Justin first attended Colonial Forge High School in Stafford, because most of his AAU baseball friends were going there. Shelia explained that *"Justin later transferred to North Stafford because rides became a problem to Forge, and he had made other good friends who were going there. So after a semester, off he went to North. During his sophomore year, about two months before he was diagnosed with cancer, Justin complained of chest pains. His pediatrician gave him a good exam but found nothing. I asked for a referral to a cardiologist, but they found nothing as well. No chest x-rays were done though. He started showing signs of swollen glands, and apparently the cancer that was later discovered, had started to move from his upper chest into his neck. The strange thing was, is that Justin was in a rehab session for* an injured knee when it was discovered. He had a sudden shortness of breath, and was taken to the emergency room."

Shelia went on to explain the turn of events as Justin's cancer was diagnosed. She said, *"it was June of 2006, and Justin was sixteen years old. At Prince William Hospital, he was given a chest x-ray. It was then that a tumor was discovered. He was rushed from Prince William to Inova Fairfax Hospital, where treatments began. A biopsy was done in his neck, and bone marrow samples were sought for testing. As strong as my own faith was, I have to be honest and say that facing Justin's cancer tapped all my personal resources. The night before his biopsy was done, I will never forget that look in Justin's eyes as he said, "momma, please don't tell me it's cancer." All I could muster was to say that if it was cancer, that God will take care of it for you. I told him that God made us Justin, and if it is cancer, he will fix you. Justin was so scared but he listened to every word. I think because his faith was so very strong, he believed that God would heal him. From that point on, Justin and I would always pray together because really, we had no idea what we were facing as a family. I was with him when they did the biopsy in his neck, and I stared into his eyes and knew he was in pain during the procedure, but he never expressed it. He had tears welling up in his eyes, but he just braced his arms and let the doctors and nurses do what they had to do. Dr. Weil easily got a bone marrow sample from his right side, but had great difficulty with the left. Justin was wearing his Superman boxers, and that is where that story really took off. Dr. Weil remarked how much milk Justin must be drinking for his bones to be so strong that she could not get the marrow from his left side so easily. What was amazing to me was seeing Justin in so much pain as these procedures were done, and he looked at me with sad eyes and sad, "don't worry momma, everything is going to be o.k." Here was a young boy telling me everything was going to be fine. That told me right then how special Justin really was."*

There was profound sadness in Shelia's eyes, that seemingly moved far away from her worries and initial concerns about Justin's diagnosis of cancer. She paused momentarily and said, *"I was so worried about Justin after his diagnosis, that it occurred to me during this time, how much time Jordie was alone by himself. I couldn't even imagine all the things he was worried about as the little brother. I would call all the time and tell Jordie of the things that were going on with Justin, but I was also so worried because I couldn't be there a lot of the time. Like*

Justin though, Jordie too would reassure me that he was fine and told me not to worry. There was one thing he said though, that was amazing. Jordie said that when he first went to see Justin, he saw several angels surrounding his bed. Jordie was very clear about what he saw, and I let him go on and tell me more. He said he knew them by name, and at one point, he told Justin where they were in the room. Jordie told me that until Justin was diagnosed with cancer, he had never seen angels before. Once he got to the hospital though, he saw them clearly. I was absolutely amazed but also very sure that Jordie did see those angels. His faith was strong and I know he would not say something like that, if they did not appear before him."

As Justin was emotionally dealing with his newly discovered cancer, Shelia said that sometimes he would call her in the middle of the night from the hospital. Shelia said, *"many nights he would call at 12:30 or 1:00 a.m., and just asked me to pray with him. He would either tell me he couldn't sleep, or he was in so much pain that he couldn't sleep if he wanted to. There was one night when he called to say that he was disturbed about a dream he had. He was dreaming that someone asked him a question of, "if cancer had to be there, would you want to take it for yourself, or have it be Jordie?" In the dream Justin answered, "let it happen to me. I don't ever want anything happening to Jordie."* Shelia said that as Justin told her this, at first she was startled about how the dream arose within Justin, but was never surprised about his response. To Shelia, and in fact, everyone else who ever had any contact with Justin Whitaker, they already knew what his answer would be.

You could see within Shelia's eyes, that she constantly drifted back in time to those sad, endless days as Justin fought his illness. He received chemotherapy for a nine month span, and the cancer went into remission. Sadly, by November of 2007, the cancer had returned in force. It was then that a bone marrow transplant was decided upon, with everyone realizing that this may be Justin's last chance in sustaining life. Shelia said,

"Justin was taken to the Children's Hospital in Washington, D.C., and was basically there for about four weeks. Justin held the distinction of being the first child to be transferred into the new wing at Children's, as they prepped him for the bone marrow transplant. For two weeks, Justin received massive doses of chemo, and radiation treatments before they could even do the transplant." Shelia also wanted to recognize the fact that as of that time, the donor of bone marrow for

Justin could not be identified. One full calendar year had to pass before the identity of that person was known. In November of 2008, Shelia said, *"I will be excited to find out the name of the person who was so generous in trying to give Justin a new lease on life."* Doctors had briefed the family before the procedure, and told the Whitakers that it was only a 50/50 chance that Justin would survive the transplant. To Shelia, *"that was the hardest piece of news to swallow."*

The doctors at Children's Hospital, remained in contact with Dr. Weil from Inova Fairfax at every turn. Shelia, like Craig, commented on Dr. Weil's incredible compassion for Justin from the first moment he was diagnosed with cancer. The nursing staff was *"absolutely amazing too,"* according to Shelia. When speaking of Dr. Marcie Weil, Shelia remarked, *"this woman was beyond wonderful. She honestly loved Justin from the very beginning. I felt the comfort zone that Justin himself felt, whenever Dr. Weil explained a procedure, or told Justin exactly what was going on. She was just a perfect, peaceful fit for what Justin was enduring. I held great confidence that Dr. Weil was the ideal person to handle Justin's cancer treatments. I remember at the funeral service how she said that she "loved Justin like he was my own child." She was so special, and we are indebted to her for her loving care of Justin."*

During my conversations with Craig, Courtney, and his best bud Zac, I came to understand the impact that Justin also had on other much younger cancer patients at Inova. Shelia concurred, and said that Justin seemed to have a magical effect on all the kids there. Shelia said, *"even when Justin was so very sick, and couldn't get out of bed, the small children also suffering from cancer, would use scooters to move through the hallway and visit him. It was so sad to see a parent holding them on the scooters sometime, as they pushed their medicine beside them, but they made the trip just to say hello to Justin. Sometimes it would be midnight, and a small child who was awake like Justin, would roll up at the entrance of Justin's door, and simply wave to him."* As Craig also mentioned, Lisa Linares was one of those special patients who became instantly aligned with Justin. Shelia thought that at the time, Lisa was six years old and that she suffered from some form of cancer near her brain stem.

As Shelia recalled the fostering of friendship between Justin and Lisa, she had to pause for a moment to take a breath. I noticed that her eyes welled up in tears, but she went on to explain 'why' this little girl came to mean so much to Justin, and vice versa. Shelia said, *"when Justin was first admitted into Inova Fairfax, I went to the gift shop and was looking for something to cheer him up. I saw this stuffed white bear with a note that said,* **"I have plans for your life. I have not forgotten you."** *It was as if God was speaking to Justin, and I felt it was perfect for him. The next day I saw little Lisa walking down the hall with her mother. She stopped just to peer into Justin's room and wave. He had the North Stafford baseball players in there with him, but stopped talking to say hello to Lisa. This was their first hello. Lisa was carrying what she described as her "favorite Barbie doll." Lisa softly said, "bye, I'm heading back to my room." The players left a short time later, and Justin and I walked out to sit on the bench in the hallway. He said, "momma, I would love to get Lisa a present." We walked back into his room, and he picked out the white bear I had given him. Lisa's mother had told me that one night, Lisa was crying to God and asked "why did God forget me?" Lisa's mother, Danicela, tried to assure her that God had not forgotten her, yet Lisa was still so sad. Justin took that bear down the hall and found Lisa, and the two of them sat on the bench together. Justin told Lisa, "I just want you to know that God has not forgotten you Lisa. He loves you." I had tears in my eyes as Justin reached out to hand Lisa the bear. Lisa had been through waves of chemo and had no hair, and it was a moment in time I will never forget."*

As Shelia told me that story, it was clearly plunging her back to the past, into that same hallway where she watched as Justin and Lisa first sat and talked. She was overwhelmed with pain all over again, and began to tear up as those same visions of that day were replayed in her mind. What Justin was not ready for, was when Lisa turned to Justin and offered him her "favorite Barbie doll." Shelia remarked, *"Lisa said, "when you get lonely, and you are all alone, you can look at this doll and think of me. But be careful, because her shoes keep falling off!"* Amidst tears in her eyes, Shelia told me that it was one of the most moving things she had ever seen. Shelia was able to smile and laugh with me, especially when she recalled Lisa making the comment about her Barbie doll, with the propensity for losing her shoes!

Shelia went on to speak of the countless hours spent at the hospital as well. She mentioned that before Justin began his chemo treatments, he was the *"same old Justin."* One long day into night, Shelia said that rather than to shower in another area, she decided to use Justin's bathroom and take a shower there. As she finished Shelia said, *"I was drying off and thought I could hear Justin talking to someone. I then heard him say, "mom, I think you know who I am talking to." Once again, I thought that he was speaking to me now, and as I stepped from the bathroom, I saw that Justin's eyes were completely closed as he laid still. I never said a word and sat right down next to him for about fifteen minutes. I just sat and watched him at rest, curious as to what I had heard. He then slowly opened his eyes and looked at me. I asked him who he was talking to. He said, "I was talking to Jesus mom. As soon as you opened the door from the bathroom into the room, he left." Again, I knew that Justin was telling the truth, and felt his faith stronger than ever. Then two weeks later, I had fallen asleep in Justin's room, and woke up to find him sitting straight up in bed. I asked him what was wrong, and he said, "the door to my room kept opening by itself." I glanced over at the door to see it slightly opened. I got up and closed it. Justin was never scared, but he did say that it was not the first time it happened."*

The entire time Shelia and I talked, our conversation returned to Justin's immense faith, and spiritual strength. Shelia remarked that, *"Justin always held a high faith that he would beat his cancer and get better. He talked of fighting all the way through it. In November of 2007, he came down with mouth sores that were so bad, he could barely swallow or eat. Then in February of 2008, Justin was in extreme pain and turned to me and said, "momma, my body can't keep handling this type of treatment." He was in agony. The doctors told us in November after the bone marrow transplant failed, that they had no idea how long Justin had to live. They would constantly tell us to instill within Justin thoughts of "living his life now the best he can." Justin and I had one quiet, special, emotional moment during this span of time. I looked at him, knowing he was in so much pain and simply asked, "Justin, I need to know that if you fall asleep, and God calls on you, are you ready to go home?" Justin looked at me and said, "mom, I love Jesus with all my heart. If he calls my name, I am ready to go home. Since we were young, you taught us about Jesus. That is why I can be so strong now."* Reliving this event was too much for Shelia to handle, and she broke down and cried as she finished telling me what Justin had said to her. I think that is why I was so taken aback by the poem written by Kathryn James, lamenting the loss of her son Matthew at the beginning of this chapter when she wrote, *"his mission here is finished. Our father called him home."* Those same words applied to the *"home"* Justin would soon be realizing, as he too would be taken to a better place, free of this dreadful pain that had ravaged his tired body.

The manner in which Shelia spoke of Justin's faith, and of his surety in the fact that he would be ready to go home if, and when the time arose, made me feel the impact of his strength and courage even more. Shelia added, *"you always wonder when you take your kids to church as parents, if they are even getting the messages…hearing the words? Do they even understand the lessons from God, and have the faith to comprehend? I honestly knew, that when Justin was in the very worst stages of pain, that he possessed full faith in God. He internalized that which had been taught to him since he was a young boy, and that acceptance readied him for death, if that is what happened. I remember in February how he looked at me and said, "momma, I am so tired. We ought to go look around* (Justin according to Shelia, was referring to picking out a burial plot)." Shelia responded with, *"Justin, I am not ready for that yet. All Justin said was, "o.k. mom," and after that he never brought it up again."*

Shelia also spoke lovingly about Justin's offer of the promise ring for Courtney. She told me the story of how she got together with two other nurses from the Inova ICU and ordered the ring on-line. Shelia said, *"Justin was so cute and proud to be picking this ring out. The nurses were so incredibly generous getting together money, and buying this ring for him. My heart was so full of joy for what they had done. The ring was delivered to the house, and I brought the ring up to Justin to show it to him. When I got to his room with the ring, I asked him what he was going to promise Courtney? He looked at me with such a sincere expression and said, "momma, I will promise to marry her someday."* I think if you knew Justin at all, you can close your eyes and feel that sentimental moment shared with his mother.

Amidst all of the pain and endless treatments, Shelia also sought to reflect on a light moment spent with Justin in the hospital. It was now the first week of March 2008, and Shelia was in Justin's room and noticed that the skin on the bottom of his feet were starting to peel. She watched as he had pulled his socks off and scratched at the dry skin. Shelia seized the moment and joked, *"what you need Justin is a pedicure! He didn't even have a clue what it was. I started helping him clean his feet and toes, and smoothing his dried skin. Justin was always this big strong guy, but when his feet turned soft and*

ON THE SEVENTH DAY OF APRIL...SUPERMAN DIED

clean, he started telling all the nurses about his now beloved pedicure. It's funny because Courtney and her softball trainer Dave Gonier, were up at the hospital visiting Justin, and Dave messed with him saying that "men don't get pedicures Justin." Justin just turned his way and with that big old smile of his said, "well, my mom just gave me one." That was the end of that!"

I had the feeling that as we started to wind down our talk, that our next discussion would center on Justin's last, bad turn. In many ways, largely because I was so taken and spellbound by Shelia's warm words about Justin, I dreaded taking her there. But again, as we talked and made eye contact, you just *knew* you were speaking with someone who never diverted from her faith. She clearly held strong, spiritual beliefs that seemingly sustained her for a lifetime. I could not even fathom going through any of this with one of my kids, but isn't that how we all view something we dread? We shifted gears and talked about Justin's return home from that promise ring weekend at Virginia Beach, shared with Courtney, and the Crews family.

Shelia noted that, *"after Justin returned from Virginia Beach, he seemed to be very lethargic. This was the night before he went into the coma, and little did I know, it would be the last time we would communicate as mother and son. I drove over to the house. Courtney was there lying beside Justin in his room as they were relaxing, ready to watch television. I told him that I would let him get some rest, and I leaned down to hug him. This hug was very different though. As I leaned down to hug him, Courtney, who was laying on her back, rolled over away from us onto her stomach. It was almost like she knew that this had to be a special moment with Justin and I. In many ways, I really think she knew he was slipping very fast, and this hug was very different for that reason. Justin held me a little longer than normal, and said, "momma, I bought you a present from the beach. It's in the pink and white bag on the table downstairs." I told Justin I would check in with him at lunch the next day, said I loved him, and left the house. When I got home I reached into the bag and found that Justin had bought me a beautiful six inch cross with a faith stone. There was an inscription that said, "Put your hands in God's hands, and all your plans will succeed." The next morning, very early, I received a frantic call from Craig about Justin being rushed to the hospital. He was taken to Mary Washington Hospital in Fredericksburg, and later that afternoon, was transported to the Inova Fairfax ICU."*

Shelia explained that it was a harrowing few days as Justin slipped into the coma, and was lying still in his bed within the ICU. As she explained, *"it was about 6:30 or 7:00 p.m., and I told everyone to go home and get some rest. I wanted to stay the night with Justin. About an hour passed, and Justin started to convulse. I learned that when he was first rushed to Mary Washington, that he had contracted spinal meningitis. He was given injections, and that is when the decision was made to send him over to Inova for care. I can still see Justin lying there so still, wearing the cross I gave to him when he graduated. On the front it said, "Lion of Courage," and on the back it said, "Love, Mom." He also had his silver and black bracelet on, that was given to him by Jordie and Amber, signed, "Sis and Jordie." It was so difficult to have those removed, but the ICU nurses said it was necessary once Justin was put on life support."*

No matter who I have talked to about Justin since I began writing this book, each and every person said that they could not imagine having to make the decision to remove life support from one of their children. It is readily understood that a child dying before their parents is against the natural order of things, yet to be the one having to make a decision such as this, is something far too surreal to fathom. Talking to Shelia about this, you could not help but to feel that the decision to click Justin's machine off, was absolutely based on her feelings that Justin was truly ready to *"go home."* Shelia explained that, *"Craig and I were with Dr. Weil and those closest to Justin, and I turned to Craig and said that Justin was ready to go. Dr. Weil explained that from the moment that the unit supporting Justin's life was shut down, the time of his death could be anywhere from twenty to forty five minutes or so. All I asked was that the doctors and nurses continuously played this music that I had brought into Justin's room. It played the entire time Justin was on life support. It was a beautiful, serene, peaceful string of melodies that speak of one being at the feet of Jesus. Dr. Weil, the nurses, and so many other people hearing this music, all told me that no matter what they were doing, they were continuously drawn to Justin's room. They spoke of peace and serenity from not only hearing the music, but of being near Justin, and feeling closer to him."*

As the time inched closer to Justin's death, Shelia started to reflect on all that the family, and loved ones had been through for close to two years. She quietly said, *"I knew that even when Justin was in a coma, he heard my every word. His sister Amber had a special way of praying with, and for Justin* too, and there is no doubt that he heard everyone's prayers. Right after Justin's life support was shut down, I slid up on the bed with him as the first hour slowly went by. I could notice a change in his breathing, almost like he did when he was sleeping…free and easy. I put my right hand across his heart, and rested my head on his arm. I whispered, it's o.k. to go home with Jesus now. I said, you used to tell me that when you made it big, you would build me that big house. When you do go home, build my mansion next door to Jesus. That is why I chose that song ('Build My Mansion Next Door To Jesus') to sing with Aunt Dee Dee, at Justin's memorial service. I whispered those same words to Justin two more times, in the second hour, and right before he took his last breath. I stayed in the same position the entire time, right up until he did take that last breath, because I wanted Justin to feel safe knowing that he was safe now, and in the arms of God."

There were other emotions that were troubling for Shelia, as her eldest son was about to pass away. Shelia said, "I knew that I had to be there for Jordie too, as a source of comfort, so that he was not afraid. I could hear and see everyone crying around me, but I was in this incredibly peaceful state of mind. I told everyone that when Justin does reach down and draw his last breath, he will be meeting Jesus face to face. I was content in my faith, as I am sure Justin was, because I had so many deep, intimate conversations with Justin during his life. I have had friends ask me if I was mad at God, or asked me if I questioned 'why' Justin had to be taken? I told them no, and explained that I have seen how many lives Justin has touched. Even if it was only one or two people at a time, I believe because of his faith and strong convictions, he would not have it any other way. I did not want to have that traditional last goodbye with Justin, because I knew that one day, I was going to see him again."

I decided to break off the topic of Justin's tragic passing for a few minutes, and talk to Shelia about lighter times, and the moments that most touched her heart. She said that, "on Justin's birthday in September of 2007, I was wondering what would be the perfect gift for his birthday. I decided on at least a couple of praise and worship tapes. Then I went into a shop and saw this beautiful, crafted sailboat that was resting on a nice piece of granite. It had a saying on it that touched me, and somehow, I knew that God had directed me to this sailboat so that I would buy it for Justin. I bought it, and when I gave it to him, I said that God told me to tell you to see yourself on a beautiful, calm day in the most peaceful setting that you can imagine. Then out of nowhere the water gets rough and choppy, and the blue skies turned to grey. I asked Justin, if that happens, what are you prepared to do? He looked perplexed, so I answered it for him. I said, there are only two things you can do. You can talk to the person in charge of this storm, and ask that it change, or just hang on to both sides of the boat with your strong arms and ride it out. My message to Justin was that he needed to talk to God about the storm raging all around his life, and then do whatever was necessary to weather it. I still have that boat and think about that conversation, along with anything else I ever gave Justin, that carries with it the true meanings of who Justin really was as a person."

As we were wrapping up a most emotional, yet equally peaceful conversation, I asked Shelia if, on a down day, she became angry and *did* question the 'why's' as to Justin's illness and death. She firmly said, *"there are most who may question 'why' Justin was taken from us, but I wish to find comfort in the fact that Justin trusted God 100%. These past two years, he never, ever knew exactly what was coming next, but he held great faith and confidence that God would carry him through it all. Justin was not afraid to die. I truly believe that all of Justin's internal courage, and fight to live was purely faith-based. If I ever referred to him as 'Superman,' it was strictly because God gave him that strength, and for no other reason. It could not have come from anywhere else. I have never met another man my entire life, who is as strong in his heart, soul, and body as Justin. I am not saying that as a mother. It was the way he treated a woman, the kindness he displayed with all, carrying with him a sense of maturity that was far beyond his young age. Justin was the perfect example of a gentleman, who first and foremost, placed his faith in God. In a short span of time, he managed to live his life to the fullest. He planted a seed that touched many lives. I truly feel it was God's plan to offer Justin incredible strength and faith, that in turn, allowed him to touch others in life, that may not have been able to be touched."* As we said goodbye on this particular day, for one of the first times in my life, I was rendered speechless. When I began driving away, my phone rang. It was Shelia who said that she forgot to tell me something. She said, *"I wanted to tell you that for my last birthday, Justin gave me a Celine Dion disc with the song 'Because You Loved Me' on it, which I loved. It's a beautiful song that I can listen to now and bring him back."* I knew the song well, and as we talked on the phone, in my mind I heard some of the verses come back to me. One of them seemed ever so fitting…

You were my strength when I was weak

ON THE SEVENTH DAY OF APRIL...SUPERMAN DIED

You were my voice when I couldn't speak
You were my eyes when I couldn't see
You saw the best there was in me
Lifted me up when I couldn't reach
You gave me faith 'coz you believed
I'm everything I am
Because you loved me

Part of me by now, knew that in almost everything I had discovered about Justin Whitaker since I embarked on writing a story about the magical ways in which he touched so many people, even a verse within a beautiful song held reminders of him. On this gorgeous day as I drove my truck and daydreamed, this simple song flowed through my mind. In Justin, we were all gifted to have been warmed by his presence.

As a touching postscript to Kathryn James losing contact with two brothers, and one sister since 1960, in late October of 2008, Kathryn sent me a note explaining that all of her siblings had now been located. There is hope that they will reunite soon, yet Kathryn in her note, sullenly wished that her brothers and sisters *"had the chance to meet her Matty."* Somehow, I believe that through her words and faith, they already have met.

From the Moment of That First Hello

Courtney Crews first met Justin Whitaker when they were both twelve years old, and fittingly, it was on a baseball diamond. The bad thing for the lanky number seven, was that Courtney was a pitcher facing him in a Stafford County youth game and, she unceremoniously struck him out. When recently talking to Courtney about that infamous strikeout of number seven, she said that right after that, and whenever it was ever brought up again, Justin would always say, *"I swung at those pitches because I felt bad for you."* She said they always had laughs about that for years. Knowing Justin as I did just a couple years later, I am quite sure he did not take that very well. Even at that young age, Courtney later spoke of Justin being protective of her when they both played together on a travel baseball squad. Craig Whitaker recalled those days well, and said that whenever a rival player, or anyone on her team teased Courtney, you would always see Justin stepping in and squaring away any issues they had. Courtney added that this was the time in their lives when she and Justin began to really bond. Their twelve year old Stafford County All-Star team took fourth in the state, and at that time, it was the highest position tallied by any SBL team in Virginia.

Val Crews, Courtney's mother, also reflected on meeting Justin during the Stafford Baseball League season of 2003. Steve, Courtney's father, recalled how Courtney was so excited about striking Justin out, but their bond of friendship had not even begun to truly root yet. Val and Steve remembered how Justin became Courtney's protector on the all star squad. Val said, *"Justin wouldn't let opposing team players say anything to Court, or about her, and he really impressed us with the respect he had for her as not only a ballplayer, but simply because she was the only girl on the team. Justin had the biggest heart, and he truly had more respect for others around him, than anyone I could remember at his age. During this same time, we had the privilege of meeting Justin's father Craig, his brother Jordie, and his grandparent's Barb, and Darrell.*

ON THE SEVENTH DAY OF APRIL....SUPERMAN DIED

We all had such fun watching games together at the Virginia State tournament. I am so happy my mother got to meet Justin then too. She adored him as much as the rest of our family did. We actually have a picture of Justin giving Courtney a high five as the team lined up during the tournament. After baseball ended that year, we really didn't see the Whitaker's around that much. Justin went off to Rodney Thompson Middle School, and Court went to H.H. Poole. Everyone got pretty busy."

Steve Crews also holds vivid memories of that warm summer of SBL All Star baseball when he first had the privilege of meeting Justin Whitaker. Steve said that *"right after Court and Justin were chosen as all stars, I met Justin and had my first face-to-face during the playoffs. I think what impressed me the most, is that he looked me in the eyes when he spoke to me. He was very respectful, had good manners, and just genuinely struck me as an honest young man. Courtney was the only girl that we saw playing through both regional and state playoffs, and I never forgot how Justin and another teammate took Court under their wings. We got to know Justin's dad and grandparents well during the games. Justin's grandparents were retired Air Force folks, so we had a lot in common."*

Val and Steve also discussed family times, and how Justin first meshed into the Crews household. Val said that, *"the first day that I saw Justin rollerblade over to our house to visit Court, he became a part of our family."* Steve added, *"it was funny but Justin just so happened to be rollerblading by when Courtney was outside in the front yard. They both assured me that it was strictly a coincidence, but it continued happening every day. Each hello seemed to last a little longer every day. Eventually, it got to the point that it would turn too dark outside for Justin to rollerblade home, so I ended up giving him rides. I was worried about his safety, but those rides gave me the chance to really get to know him one-on-one. I found that over time, sometimes Justin and I would talk about more things than I did with my own son Trevor. That is not knocking Trev, it's just the way things go sometimes between a father and son I guess. But those times talking with Justin made him something more uncommon and special in my eyes."* Val spoke more of those first rollerblading hellos, saying, *"that (rollerblading treks) was only days after Court and Justin had reunited with each other at a high school football game. Justin was so polite, nice, and very talkative. I had to step outside just to let him know Mom was home...ha! To be honest, after that, I never even thought of having to do that again. That day, I watched Justin and Court throw the baseball outside, and later they went rollerblading together. He even helped her with homework. Justin was definitely every mom and dad's dream as a special young man to be Courtney's good friend. Courtney's trainer, Dave Gonier, was a special mentor to both Justin and Court, calling them "best buds." Dave thought Justin was the ideal person for our little girl. Justin was so much fun to be around and so full of life. He was always watching out for his little brother Jordie too. Little did Court and Justin know, but Jordie was our special chaperone if the three of them went out together. That was always a fun joke with Steve and I."*

It was abundantly evident how much Steve Crews in time, came to know and respect Justin Whitaker, and through his own words, loved him as if he *were* his own son. Steve paused to reflect on a young man whose presence remained deep inside of him. In quiet contemplation Steve said, *"when I was Justin's age, and I think most teenagers today feel this way, parents are just not cool! I remember things that I would not dare to discuss with my mother and father. But, I do remember a time when I was Justin's age, and I knew I could always talk to a man named Stuart Woolcott. I felt as if I could talk to him about anything, and I hoped one day that I could be as cool as he was when I had my own kids. I know kids in general have not changed all that much, but I shared the same relationship with Justin as I did with Mr. Woolcott. My relationship with Justin never changed much after his cancer diagnosis. He was comfortable enough with me to talk about anything. Justin and I spoke openly and honestly through his whole ordeal. Occasionally, he would ask me what I would do in his place? All I could come up with is what my dad instilled in me as I was growing up. I said, Justin, you just have to trust in God and fight the good fight. His faith in God was always so strong, and seemed to grow deeper through each and every disappointment. He was always more concerned about others. He had an infectious smile, and an inspiring demeanor, regardless of his medical situation. I think the only time I really saw him more upset than mad, would be when he was ever delayed in leaving the hospital after treatments. Justin just wanted to go home. It was important for him to get back home and see his family, and close friends. It truly buoyed his outlook to be able to do the normal things that teenagers do."*

It seemed that virtually everyone I talked to about Justin Whitaker, spoke of his absolute love for sports. Val Crews was no different. Val said that she would often hear Justin and Court spar about *everything* in sports. Val said, *"they would talk about who had the best teams, which players would get* traded, who made the best plays...and on and on it would go. It got to the point where we gave them a sports trivia game just to see who **really** was the best, which was entertainment all by itself. Sports aside though, no matter where we were, Justin was always about making sure that Courtney was taken care of, and ladies were always first. Even if Justin came over to the house for dinner, we would tell him "guests first Justin," when it related to being served. He would always protest right away and say, "please Mrs. Crews, ladies first." He would always wait for Court and I to be served first. How could you say no to this young man with such a kind, giving heart?"

Val Crews, in many of her comments, came right back to speak about Justin's beloved ballpark. There was never any confusion about J.W.'s love of the diamond. Val said, *"even if Justin was with us when we went to watch Court play a game, or any other, before he would head to the snack bar, he would always ask if we wanted anything. If you said no, he would bring something back for you anyway, just in case you had changed your mind. One thing I always remember about Justin is that every time he would go to the snack bar, he would always get Court a bag of M&M's for after the game...or just because. At the games Justin was so much fun. He would sit there and tell us what pitch was coming next and would always be right. He may not have liked some of the umpire's calls, but he knew the game so well. We always loved having Justin with us at games, regardless of what sport it was. He was Court's number one fan, and she loved that. Sometimes at Court's basketball games, Justin may arrive a little later than us. He would always come say hello to us first, and sit with us for a quarter, or maybe the entire game, before he would leave and say hello to friends. He was just so polite and such a pleasure to be around. What I choose to remember about Justin is, he was not just special as an individual. He always made everyone around him feel special too."*

Courtney clearly remembers the date of September 10th their freshman year, when North Stafford played Colonial Forge in football. She and Justin were both fourteen at the time, and to Courtney, this was the day they *officially* became boyfriend and girlfriend. In a very funny story, Courtney related to me that her father Steve put a little fright into Justin's little world when they first started dating. He strolled around a corner and handed Justin what appeared to be quite the official document entitled, *'Application To Date My Daughter.'* Never at a loss for words, Justin first looked stunned, and then laughed with all and in complete parental disdain, refused to sign the form. Steve Crews *officially* let him slide on that one! When sitting down with Courtney in July of 2008, three months had passed since Justin's death. She was clearly reflecting back in time and softly remarked, *"we would always say that between my family and the Whitaker's, we always had one family and two houses. My father was crushed by Justin's death, and said that losing Justin, was like losing his own son."* On a side note, Craig Whitaker asked Steve Crews to speak at Justin's memorial service, but Steve declined, saying that he felt that it would be far too emotional, and difficult to even speak. I could tell by comments from Val why that was. Justin seemed to invoke those emotions from everyone.

Val and Steve Crews knew all too well of Justin's love of baseball, but as they got to know him better over time, they also learned of his love of history. Val remarked about how Justin would constantly question Steve about anything and everything to do with history. Val said, *"Justin was so knowledgeable about historical facts, and he would constantly ask Steve questions about subjects that ranged from how many soldiers fought in different wars, to the aircraft used in them. I enjoyed watching Justin and Steve wage a war, as they quizzed each other trying to gain an upper hand. Justin always talked about "Granddad Whitaker" and his days as a pilot. He would tell us stories about his life and times."* Steve recalled the historical trivia battles with Justin as well. He said, *"Justin was always a big history buff, and with me, he would play a version of "stump the dummy" when he came over to spend time with Courtney. Needless to say, I was typically the dummy! Those were the best of times with Justin."*

In November of 2005, Val said that Justin accompanied their family to the Pentagon for a ceremony commemorating Steve's retirement. Val remarked that, *"Justin was thrilled as he looked around at all of the history surrounding him there. As I think back to that now, I am just so happy that we were able to not only open him up to the historical side of things there, but to have him present during the retirement ceremony. It was such a special occasion for our family."*

Sadly, Val and Steve forlornly talked of Justin's cancer, that was first detected after he suffered a knee injury while playing basketball. Val said, *"as you watched Justin, his illness never stopped him from doing as much as he could. We knew that he was terribly frustrated about his knee injury and having to wear a brace, but he never let that stop him from doing everything humanly possible to ready himself for another upcoming baseball season. I remember when he was going* through rehabilitation on his knee, and he started to complain about his throat bothering him. He would say "forget about my knee, I just want this lump in my throat to go away." He would come over to the house, and sit on the couch with Courtney while their friends were all out doing things. We would put a warm cloth on his throat, and he would always have this re-assuring way about him by saying, "it's o.k. Mrs. Crews." He would thank me and all I could say was, it's no problem Buddy. I always called him that. We all felt awful because Justin was so frustrated, and didn't know what was going on with his throat. He never wanted to seem as a bother to anyone, but when we did fuss over him, he would **always** have that smile on his face that we loved...that little, quirky smirk."

Justin's physical woes became worse, and as time moved on, his frustrations mounted as he had difficulty breathing, and nobody seemed to know exactly what was going on. Val commented that, *"you could see this frustrated expression on Justin's face as it was more and more difficult to breathe, and all he wanted was answers. He always wondered whether it was a sinus infection, or tonsils, but most of all he just wanted to know what the heck was going on. He could not understand why antibiotics would not make him feel better. Justin had a physical therapist appointment for treatment on his injured knee the next day, but during the rehab session, his breathing became more distressed. He was taken to Potomac Hospital as a result, and after a chest x-ray, his cancer was diagnosed."*

Val and Steve Crews reflected on the enormity of their sadness as a family, as Justin's symptoms grew worse, and cancer was determined to be the culprit. Sadly, Val said, *"all Justin wanted was for doctors to find out what was happening to him, so that they could fix it, and he could move on doing what he loved the most...playing baseball. He wanted to feel better so he and Court could share a fun summer watching each other play ball, and then get ready for his sister's wedding in a couple of weeks. He was so excited about having the chance to walk his sister down the aisle and give her away. That was going to be a special time for he and Jordie. The special gift about Justin was, there were always lots of things going on in his mind, but his concerns seemed to center around someone else's happiness...never his. The happiness of loved ones, is what made **him** the happiest."*

The pains within Steve Crews were truly palpable as he paused to reflect on Justin's illness, and ultimately, his passing. Steve said, *"as I think about my feelings now, I realize how tough it was. I truly believe that everything happening in life, happens for a reason. It is so hard for me to try and explain Justin's fight, and ultimately, losing him. To watch him endure all of the medical procedures, and to see him ache in pain, tore at my heart as if he was my own son. My faith is what sustained me throughout this whole ordeal, probably in the same manner as Justin's sustained him. Obviously, when he was initially diagnosed with cancer, it was very difficult. Then he went through the two times that his cancer came back, and we watched his rapid decline after we returned from our trip to Virginia Beach. I think the word helplessness sums up my feelings about Justin, because there was nothing I could do to make him better physically. The only times I never felt that way was when I was around him. Whether at home or in the hospital, I always tried to maintain a positive attitude. You couldn't act any other way, because that is how Justin was all the time. He brought out the best in people. As it relates to his passing, I feel so badly for Courtney because I know she is hurting so much, and sometimes feel as if there is nothing I can do to console her. I do think though, that since Justin's death, everyone close to Court has drawn closer and closer as a result."* It was clear to me that a father's grief spread to many levels, as Steve Crews reflected on his own personal senses of loss and pain.

Val also commented on her own internal feelings of sheer pain and utter helplessness, as she first learned of Justin's cancer. Val reflected on that awful day when the Crews family went to the hospital right away after Justin's diagnosis. Val said, *"when we found out about Justin's cancer, Court and I sat down on a bench to comfort each other. At first we sat quietly, then Court leaned over and hugged me, and I knew she was fighting to hold back tears. All I could think of saying to her at that very moment was that everything would be o.k., because Justin was such a fighter. I promised Court we would help him through this no matter what. I told Court that I knew she had to be strong, but that it was o.k. to cry too. We both shed tears for about a minute, and then she suddenly stood up and said, "no, Justin's not crying and I'm not either." I remember she walked right back into his room to be with him. I truly never saw tears from Court again until Justin's cancer returned, and even then, it was more anger than tears. I truly believe that the only way she got through all of the emotional swings during Justin's illness, was by being mad, not at any one thing, but at the cancer itself and how unfair it was to Justin. I think her deepest emotions and tears were shed at night when she was all alone. Sometimes we would get up and check on her in the early morning*

ON THE SEVENTH DAY OF APRIL....SUPERMAN DIED

hours, and would find her asleep on the couch. Most nights, she would choose the couch because that is where she and Justin spent so much time. Whether they were watching movies, baseball games, or just talking, that couch was her comfort zone. I think in very special ways, she felt a closeness to Justin on that couch when he was not there, cuddled up in 'their' favorite blanket."

Steve went on to speak about Justin's times in the hospital and added, *"on occasion, I used to spend the night at the hospital with Justin when other family members were unable to be there. Around nine o'clock, Justin would typically get hungry. I would fix up whatever he wanted, but usually he favored something simple like Beefaroni or Spaghettio's. About forty minutes later, it always seemed like he then wanted something salty. I would make some microwave popcorn to satisfy whatever craving he had. That would be the time when he and I would chat about anything and everything. We would watch a movie, or talk about Courtney and what was happening. It's funny but I still think about how Justin always told me that Courtney was always his number one priority. He comforted me saying that I never had to worry about her welfare when she was with him. That brings to mind a short story. When Justin's father Craig bought him his Firebird, Justin drove over to the house to show us his new prized possession. He asked me if I wanted to take it out for a spin. I said sure. I would love to take a ride with you. We drove out onto Rt. 610, and then onto I-95. I asked him to show me what the car could do. He punched the accelerator and the car sped quickly up to 70 miles per hour, but then settled there. After thirty seconds, I asked Justin if that is all the power the car had. He answered, "that's all I will ever do when Court is in the car with me."*

Val and Steve, hesitatingly talked about the phone call they received at about 1:30 a.m., from Craig about Justin's condition, and seemingly fell into a state of shock. Val said at the time, *"no way this can be happening to Justin. It is so hard to remember all the thoughts that run through your head, but we knew we had to wake Courtney, and tell her we needed to get to the hospital for Justin. We just wanted to get to the hospital to see him, and keep Court and Justin thinking positively. I remember how quiet the ride was to the hospital. We were so hopeful though, and decided that it was best to get there first, and then find out everything about Justin's illness. When we finally did arrive, I will never forget the look on Justin's face. He looked very confused, and scared, yet he also remained very hopeful and optimistic. Our reassurance was that smile of his that we always got,* and at that moment in time, it was all we needed. You know, to this day, the most wonderful thing we see in our minds, was Justin and Courtney holding hands, looking at each other, and hugging without ever saying anything. If they had each other, everything was going to be all right. They found that it was best to share all smiles and no tears. They both needed each other and when together, it was as if nobody else was in the room with them." Love shared with nary a word spoken…Justin Whitaker and Courtney Crews, as seen through the eyes of parents loving them both.

As of this writing, five months had passed since Justin's death. His nineteenth birthday would have been on September 7, 2008, and that was also never far from the minds of Steve, Val, and especially, Courtney. In my gathering of thoughts from the Crews family, I felt an inherent sense of peace and serenity. They had persevered through so much personal, and emotional pain on so many levels, yet they knew that in time's passage, wounds of the heart and soul would slowly heal. Val remarked, *"I do believe that time does heal all wounds. I truly have seen Courtney move forward taking baby steps, and I knew that the time waiting in the summer to begin classes and start softball training at Hofstra, was very tough on her. I think she was really excited to go, but as the date neared, she found it difficult to leave. I believe Court harbors a lot of emotions about leaving the area, but she has begun to move forward. I think for Steve and I, and others who speak about Justin, it offers us warm memories and makes us smile. But as Courtney's mother, I have tried so many times to put myself in her shoes, and imagine what she may be feeling at any given time. I cannot even attempt to understand all of the pains within her heart. You worry not only about what she is feeling now, but what she will continue to feel when away, and alone at school. Steve and I both stand back, and admire in amazement at what our daughter has had to do. It seems funny to say, but I know that I will forever be inspired by Court's strength, and in turn, that which we learned through Justin. I believe they truly shared a love that none of us are capable of understanding. It was theirs and theirs alone, and was the type of love only they could ever understand."*

There was yet another area in which Val and Steve Crews, to this day, remain stunned over. Their pain when speaking of Justin's illness, and his rapid decline toward the end, was more than evident because their love and affection of him was immeasurable. Steve and Val felt that, *"the*

ON THE SEVENTH DAY OF APRIL…SUPERMAN DIED

hardest thing to bear, and try to comprehend, were all of the hospital stays, medical procedures, injections, chemotherapy, and all of the drugs fed into Justin to counteract side effects etc. They aligned with Justin's dad Craig, when he said, *"they threw the kitchen sink at him and he kept on fighting." It was just so unfair for Justin to wage the battle that he did and not win this fight. There were so many uncertainties and turns in the road, and quite frankly, in the end, I think Justin's death made us all a little stronger." There were times when doctors were optimistic, and that made Justin stronger, and as an extension of that, everyone naturally felt better. For Justin's sake, because of such a valiant fight, I think we learned as a family to grab hold of ALL the positives in everything you do, and run with them as far as they will take you. There were times when we were left to 'wishing' good thoughts, in hope that Justin would eventually be o.k. You wished so hard, then you placed your faith and trust in God, knowing that He always knew what was best for us. That is when we all came to the understanding that our faith was all that we had, and we needed to believe in it every day."* The Crews family *did* hit the nail on the head. Justin's fight was strong, defiant, and courageous because he *did* possess the fight of a lion, and the faith of an angel. I truly believe being surrounded by those he loved, and how they loved him back, left him in a peaceful state of mind place. Yet, rest assured he *is* still sporting that devlish grin watching over all of us.

Steve vividly remembered what life was like in the Crews household just one thin week after Justin's death. Steve said, *"that first week, Courtney didn't spend one night at home. That first night, Rev. Zac Ashley from Mt. Ararat Baptist Church, spoke to Courtney and about fifteen other kids as they grieved. Initially there were tears, but it quickly turned to a remembrance of all the good times. It was important for Courtney's friends to be around during this time in many ways. I think everyone's collective support for each other, really got everybody through those very emotional times. I did notice though, as all of Court's friends started to leave for college, the key senses of support that she felt started to wane a little. She was naturally withdrawn, but equally excited as her own departure for college neared."*

Steve Crews, in similar fashion to how Courtney and all of Justin's friends remembered all of the good times, took a few moments to reflect on what his happiest memories were. Steve looked at Justin's life in totality, and solemnly remarked, *"I think back at all the baseball and softball games and smile. I think of Justin over at our house as cookies were made, of course with the accompanying flour fights. I see Justin and Court ready to go to homecomings, and proms, and just kicking back watching television. That last trip to Virginia Beach before Justin passed away though, held many lasting memories. The shame of that last trip, was how quickly Justin's health declined, and we were all hit by the realization that he truly was not going to beat his illness. Each and every moment though, when I stop and think about Justin being around, they were filled with nothing but the best of times…the absolute best of times."*

Courtney's Promise Ring

A Promise
A promise to be your lover, to be your friend
A promise that's everlasting, that will never end
A promise to stay with you through good times and bad
To make you happy, and to hold you when you're sad
A promise to take your hand in marriage and let nothing get in the way
And finally, a promise to love you every hour of every day

Jim Krzyzak (8/12/97)

This touching poem was written by Jim Krzyzak, in memory of his wife Katherine McCloughan-Krzyzak, who passed away in 2002 at the tender age of twenty six. Jim gave this poem to his loving companion Kate, as he offered her a promise ring. Kate suffered from the effects of cystic fibrosis and just prior to her death, had received two lung transplants that her body ended up rejecting. As I began to pen thoughts about Justin offering a similar promise ring to Courtney, a mere two days before he slipped into a coma, I literally stumbled upon Kate's story. I was absolutely floored because of the correlation of two deeply touching, heartfelt stories. Justin and Courtney, Jim and Kate, two love-struck couples, yet each sharing similar, tragic consequences of death. I was initially searching for the meanings behind promise rings, and the poignant love and affection that they offered, and came away with so much more. When speaking with family members and friends at Justin's memorial service, everyone at some point, spoke of Justin and Courtney's trip to Virginia Beach. I listened to each version as more information was added, and a complete picture of both of them, as if you were looking at a photograph. They were at the beach for a softball tournament, and later enjoyed seafood, followed by a walk down the long, wood planked boardwalk. I think everyone who has ever known Justin can easily recall that smirk he *always* carried on his face. You just *knew* that as he readied to give Court her promise ring, Justin was absolutely bursting inside with indescribable excitement. It was an expression that told you he knew something that you clearly did not! It was amazing how Justin even managed to smile during this romantic time in his life. His boyish grin veiled the fact that he was suffering through some of the worst pain of his life. Yet, he wanted and so *needed* this beautiful moment in time shared with one he loved.

Courtney fondly recalled their trip together to Virginia Beach at the end of March 2008, when Justin bashfully took Courtney's hand and lead her across the sand, and onto a pier jutting out over the Atlantic Ocean. Their final destination found themselves in soft sand staring at each other. According to Courtney later, in typical Justin fashion, he became bashful and started speaking without any eye contact. Justin pulled out a single diamond promise ring, told Courtney how much he loved her, and that he wanted to spend the rest of his life with her. Courtney later joked after Justin's passing how he had asked, "do you want to do the same?" Ever the jokester, Courtney could not let him right off this slippery hook, and simply said in a dead panned tone, *"no."* As everyone later learned, they both started laughing, and moments later Courtney said "yes."

Val and Steve Crews often sit at home and reflect on that special trip with Courtney and Justin as well. Val said, *"Justin seemed so happy to be finally going to a beach to fulfill his dream and give Court her promise ring. He seemed very tired, but he looked pretty good. There were a few times when it seemed that he had trouble swallowing, but each time we would ask him if he was o.k., he would always say, "it's o.k. Mr. and Mrs. Crews, I'm o.k." That was Justin! Justin called it "their vacation," so he was always making sure they were doing all that they planned. He was so cute checking with Court first before making a decision. Justin was not going to let anything interfere with his moment in giving Courtney her promise ring. We remember how excited and nervous Justin was as his wish was about to come True. We were also excited for Court, because Steve and I knew she was going to be so surprised. In all honesty, we were very guarded with Justin because of his health, combined with how emotional this moment was. If he was hurting, or not feeling well* at Virginia Beach, he never showed it. We knew he had to be in a great deal of pain because he had endured so much. But, he truly was so strong...our Superman."

Just before the momentous Virginia Beach trip, Dr. Weil sat with Justin during an appointment and asked him what he wanted to do with his life. Everyone knew of Justin's dreams of going to college, playing baseball again, and rising above this terrible illness. But he chose this moment to once again unselfishly tell Marcie that all he wanted was to give the girl he loved in life, Courtney, a promise ring. Five of the staffers from Inova's ICU chipped in $50 apiece, and bought Justin's cherished white gold, diamond ring. Marcie and the nurses actually tricked Justin into believing that they were just going to help him pick out the ring, but they surprised him with the gift that Justin would later offer to Courtney. What most never knew or heard about, was that Dr. Weil had also given Justin another gift, so that the offer of this promise ring could even take place. Before the couple could revel in this romantic occasion, Marcie and Justin's self-proclaimed "personal nurse" Kelly Printz, infused him with two units of platelets that would prevent both internal, and external bleeding. Justin's father Craig said later, that had Justin not received these treatments, he would not have been able to share this cherished time with Courtney. It was quite evident that within the hospital ICU, Justin's caregivers continuously grieved over Justin's fate at every turn. Without their professionalism, generosity, and selflessness, Justin's offer of a promise ring would not have been realized.

Val and Steve Crews, spoke lovingly about Justin's special gift, one given from the heart from a young man who truly loved their daughter. Val said, *"I actually had Courtney's ring at our house for a while because Justin was afraid that Court might find it at his house. I hid it in my jewelry box and knew that Court would not look there. She never asked to wear my jewelry, and for the most part, only wore her class ring, necklaces, and a bracelet that Justin had given her. She also wore a special bracelet that Grandma and Grandpa Whitaker gave her when Justin first began his fight against cancer. Before we had left for Virginia Beach, Justin had given me the ring. I put it in a pouch within my purse where it stayed until that Saturday afternoon when the softball tournament ended. We went to Rockefeller's Restaurant for dinner, which had a beautiful blue dolphin on a pedestal outside. The dolphins bring back more memories, because Justin had always* wanted to bring Courtney to Hawaii, and give her the chance to swim with the dolphins. She had wanted to do that since she was a little girl, and Justin had the whole thing planned one day. He was never able to do that for her, but we took a nice picture of them sitting beside that blue dolphin, which was very sweet."

Steve Crews added another perspective to this momentous weekend, yet the beginnings of it, as it related to Courtney's promise ring, actually took place in Stafford, Virginia first. Steve said, *"one night when Justin was over our house watching a movie, Court left the room to go do something, and Justin slid over to talk to me. Justin asked me if he could have my permission to give Courtney a promise ring. I asked him what that would mean. He responded by saying, "it was a promise ring to marry only after we both finished college." I told him how proud I would be to have him as part of our family. I think about that brief conversation to this day."*

Val then painted a picture of going to the boardwalk, shopping, and making a romantic stop at the beach. As Val explained, *"when we pulled into the parking lot, Justin was sitting behind me in the truck. The two of us got out and Justin, very quickly and nervously said, "Mrs. Crews, did you bring the ring?" I just grinned and said yes I've got it. Steve tried to distract Courtney as I gave Justin the ring. He put it in the pocket of his letterman's jacket, and when I looked at him he was grinning ear to ear. Justin then asked Court what stores she wanted to go into, and was playing the part of the good little shopper. I remember how Justin bought things for everyone in his family, and both of them were so thoughtful. When the shopping spree was done, it was time to head down toward the pier, and ultimately, the beach. Steve and I gave them as much space as possible, but we also wanted to make sure that Court and Justin had a picture of this very special moment. I guess we were like paparazzi but much nicer! We were so thankful to have pictures from that very special night. We were two parents, so happy to be part of the lives of two wonderful people. Justin and Courtney had been through so much together, yet they still held onto the hopes and beliefs that they would someday share the rest of their lives as one. This special ring from Justin to Courtney, was a promise to wait for each other no matter what. Standing from afar on a beach, this truly was the most wonderful, memorable, amazing, loving moment we could have ever shared with Justin and Courtney. There are simply not enough words to describe it."*

Val and Steve related to me that the promise ring given at Virginia Beach, was supposed to have been originally done in Pensacola, Florida.

ON THE SEVENTH DAY OF APRIL....SUPERMAN DIED

Justin accompanied the Crews family to Florida for softball games involving Court's college, Hofstra. Val said, *"because we were going to be right on the beach, Justin was going to give Court the promise ring there, but the weather turned cold and windy. The risk of Justin becoming very ill in that weather was not even an option. Justin was very frustrated, so his special gift had to come via a detour on another softball-related trip to Virginia Beach. It's funny but this ring had multiple destinations I guess. During spring break, the 'original' plan was for Justin to give Court her ring when they arrived in Hawaii. Justin was supposed to go with Court, Justin's mom Shelia, his sister Amber, and his brother Jordie. But because of Justin's deteriorating medical condition, and the length of the flight etc., the plans had to be changed. The only plan that never changed was the one consistent theme in Justin's mind...to offer Court her ring on a beach. Steve and I think back to times when Justin was in the hospital, and he asked both of us at least a couple times, for permission to give Courtney her promise ring. It was so sweet and honorable. I guess when we think about it now, maybe Justin just wanted to know that he was going to be able, and strong enough to give it to her in the way he wanted. I guess the way he asked us allowed us to feel that moment too before it even happened. It gave us all hope."*

Steve weighed in on the whole weekend at Virginia Beach, well before Justin was going to give Courtney her ring. Steve said, *"I remember a chilly, blustery morning at Princess Anne High School in Virginia Beach. We were all sitting behind the backstop during the games. Justin was bundled up in a hoodie, his letterman's jacket, and a couple of blankets. I think it was the first time the entire season he had been able to see Court play. I looked over at him and saw that he had his head tilted back in his chair with his eyes closed. I leaned over toward him, thinking that maybe he wasn't feeling well, and wanted to make sure he was o.k. At that point, Justin opened his eyes and looked right at me and said, "do you know how long it's been since I've been able to do this Mr. Crews?" I asked him, do what Justin, watch Court play? He said, "no sir, just being outside able to feel the sun on my face. I have really missed being able to do simple things like that." That is what made Justin so special. He was always able to find joy in the little things that most of us take for granted. As far as softball went, Courtney had been in a little slump, but that game she went three for four, with two doubles and a triple. Justin loved watching Court play, and they talked about the games for the rest of that afternoon."*

Steve recalled that after Justin gave Courtney her ring, they all made their way back to the motel. Steve said, *"Justin decided it was time to have Spaghettio's, so I made a bowl for him. We all had decided to watch a movie, and about forty five minutes later, we made some popcorn and relaxed. I will never forget that as we sat around, Justin got this real serious look on his face. He turned and looked me right in the eyes and asked me if "I knew how happy Courtney had made him on that beach?" All I could say was that I could only imagine. I told him about the night in Savannah, Georgia when I proposed to Val. The way Justin said that to me was very special."* Steve passed onto me what I had already known. Justin Whitaker was a rare breed for such a young man. He cared not for pretenses, or false impressions, because the root of his kindness emanated from a place in his heart that made everyone feel loved and good about themselves. His inner happiness came as a result of your own.

Since Justin's passing, Steve and Val commented about Courtney's promise ring, and how near and dear it is to her no matter what she is doing, or where she may be. Val said, *"since Justin gave her that promise ring, Court kept it with her everywhere she went. If she couldn't wear it because she was practicing, or playing ball games, she would keep it in it's original box in a special place right there near the field. Steve and I feel that Courtney's promise ring is also her stepping stone in a way. As we watched from afar after Justin's death, we saw Court move forward in small steps. We noticed that sometimes she would not wear her ring for a day or two. Then we would see her wearing the ring, yet during these times she seemed to stay close to home. To us, it was almost like she was trying to decide if it was o.k. to move forward in life without feeling guilty. This is what I meant earlier when I spoke of putting myself in Court's shoes, and trying to desperately understand what she has been feeling all of this time. It is just impossible! She coveted that promise ring as she took it with her to Hofstra. The quiet, baby steps she is taking as her life moves forward has made her stronger. We know that in her heart, Justin's promise ring gives her that strength, and makes her feel safe…keeping him forever close to her. We noticed a recent spark to her voice as classes began, and her training in softball intensified. Her conversations now include laughter, and her trademark jokes. To us, she sounded like the same old Courtney…driven, determined…blessed."*

The general plan for both Justin and Courtney, was to finish high school and college, and then plan their marriage. Akin to the words of Jim

ON THE SEVENTH DAY OF APRIL....SUPERMAN DIED

Krzyzak in his promise ring poem to Kate, Courtney had in essence, promised to stay with Justin *"through good times and bad."* One week later it would become quite clear that Justin and Courtney would not share college experiences together, nor would they become blessed in church at their wedding. Courtney, the standout catcher at North Stafford High School, moved slowly forward to school and softball at Hofstra University. As she ventured in trepidation toward her future, inside she silently grieved, knowing her life would now evolve without Justin by her side. It was almost hard to fathom for those who saw Justin at Virginia Beach on their 'Promise Ring' weekend, that his life was coming to a close. So many remarked that during this special weekend, he never looked happier...so full of inner joy. Two thin days later this vibrancy would pass, as Justin slipped into a coma. The timing of this beautiful moment on a sandy beach, turned tragically dark. Courtney in her strength and remembrance of Justin, told those closest to her that she and Justin held great faith in the fact that all would be fine, and all of their dreams would one day be realized. After Justin's death, I saw Courtney many times at area baseball games, and came away amazed at the strength of this bright, cheerful eighteen year old. In many ways, you could say that Courtney and Justin were twin-like in personality. When those around them were in pain and struggling, they were both far more concerned for *them*. You can almost hear Justin say over and over now that you *"never give up."* When Courtney saw friends grieving at Justin's memorial service, she consoled each and every one of them, asking if *"they were o.k."* The 'Promise Ring' seemingly took on so much more meaning in her life now, for it symbolized true love, and a profound sense of sincerity that others may simply take for granted. That would never be the case for Courtney Crews.

Val and Steve spoke glowingly about their daughter's immense strength and character, especially considering that she *was* only eighteen years old, bearing so many traumatic, emotional burdens. They both concurred that to put one spin on how Courtney was able to keep everything together was impossible. Val did say, and Steve agreed, that *"Court drew a tremendous amount of strength within from her faith, and the manner in which she watched Justin fight. We truly believe that Justin and Courtney did talk about all of the possibilities, and the ways in which his cancer may go, but every step of the way their senses of hope never wavered. They were twins in many regards. If she was down, then Justin could sense it and vice versa. There were times when Justin was sick, and he would call her at home when she was doing homework on her computer. Court would always prioritize being by Justin's side in person, but when she couldn't and he called, she would click her speaker phone on, and talk as she worked. During the really bad times, especially when the bone marrow transplant failed, it was so difficult for Steve and I not to rush Court up to be with Justin. But, she had to get all her studies done, and nobody understood that more than Justin. He was so proud of her, and all he ever wanted to do was go to New York and Hofstra, and see where Court was going to go to school and play softball. He was cheated from doing that. Even though he never made the trip, he did get to meet Court's coaches, and it was so touching to see the picture of them wearing Justin's shirt. He was able to see the Hofstra softball team and coaches wearing his shirt during warm ups in a game against Baylor in Florida. It was so very touching."*

Returning once again to the Krzyzak family and Kate's equally tragic death, I looked over a beautifully moving website remembering Kate's life and times. In one simple, short entry, her husband Jim made a poignant statement within an open email that made you ache, and align with all those suffering from Justin's loss as well. In the verse Jim wrote about Kate saying, *"she had a lot of fight in her, but this last battle was too much for her.* **Sometimes the body is weaker than the soul."** I chose to bold print that because in that simple line, it tugs at the deepest roots of your emotions, and paints the picture of both Kate and Justin. In both tragic situations, family members made the most difficult decision cast upon them...that of removing life support from someone they loved.

Kate's family members spoke of how she always wanted to *live.* Justin's family members and close friends echoed those same words. Justin's heart drummed on for close to four hours after life support was extinguished, as a final sign to all of his strength and resiliency. Friends talked of Kate and how she sought to *"conquer the world."* Superman Whitaker did as well, but as Jim Krzyzak painfully expressed, *"sometimes the body* **is** *weaker than the soul."* During Kate McCloughan's final few hours of life, her husband Jim wrote two final poems as part of a collection he had written since they met. The last two poems written bedside, contained the sentences of *"How am I supposed to continue without you by my side?"* and, *"Hold on to the strength you have given me, but I'm afraid that a part of me has died."* Justin's words of *"never give up,"* and Kate's triumphant chant of her *"readiness to conquer the world,"* are shining examples of *why* we must cherish each breath, and treasure each loving memory. Two precious souls…two promise rings binding loved ones together…forever.

"He Touched People He Never Even Knew"

"Therefore we do not lose heart. Though outwardly we are wasting away, yet inwardly we are being renewed day by day. For our momentary troubles are achieving for us an eternal glory that far outweighs them all. So we fix our eyes not what is seen, but on what is unseen. For what is seen is temporary, but what is unseen is eternal."
2 Corinthians 4:16-18

Margaret Lowry, the Athletic Director at North Stafford High School, was more than accurate saying that Justin *"touched people he never even knew."* Margaret was always amazed that regardless of the tremendous, debilitating pain he was in at times, those around him came away somehow feeling stronger. Justin was injected with five different types of chemotherapy, and even if he felt highly nauseous and weak, he would force a smile to somehow put you at ease. If you were lucky enough to be blessed with the real Justin persona, you may witness a spin of his ball cap to the rear, a set of crossed eyes staring back at you, and a tongue pointed in your direction for good measure. It is difficult to imagine that this man-child, withstanding so much pain and bodily discomfort, would lean into his dad and whisper words that basically amounted to him asking him to keep a secret regarding the *true* pain he was in. He simply did not want anyone to worry about him. He would much rather get into conversations about other people and problems they may be having, and deftly escape from his own medical woes.

Justin held onto a steadfast belief that he would one day stand back in that batter's box, and like his idol Mickey Mantle sporting that grand number seven, he would stare out at the mound, and dare you to get him out. Pause for a minute and ask yourself what is the biggest problem, or plaguing issue you are dealing with in your life right now? Then grasp those thoughts and treat that matter as if you had one day left on this earth to solve that problem, or dilemma! Justin's North Stafford baseball coach, Jim Labrusciano, said it best by saying that anytime his body aches, and he feels the need to complain, he simply closes his eyes and brings Justin Whitaker back. Jim honored Justin by softly speaking at his memorial service, and reflected on how much pain Justin was in, yet the entire time *"he never, ever flinched."*

    It's natural when we are all young men and women, that we carry ourselves in ways that make us all *appear* to be invincible, amidst a swagger that nothing can ever hurt us, or take us out of this game of life. With a lifetime in a law enforcement career, I have often been the one who held the unenviable task of driving a police unit to a perfect stranger's house, making contact with a parent, and sadly informing them that their son or daughter had been involved in a terrible accident. There were times, quite frankly, that I already *knew* that their loved one had died, yet I could not bear to deliver such sad news at their homes. I would offer instead to serve as an escort to the emergency room, where other medical professionals broke the news, and family members could be there to stand by their sides as they grieved.

    Because of Justin's ability to fight his illness at every turn, everyone on the periphery felt that in the end, he would be victorious, and beat this vicious enemy that had invaded his body. At the end of January 2008, Justin's ever loyal, and loving girlfriend Courtney, worked with North Stafford teachers in arranging a dinner and talent show to raise money for Justin's cause. Somehow, the dedicated staff at North Stafford, and those closest to Justin were able to get everything set for the dinner and show set for February 2, 2008. The crowd grew to over 500 people, arriving in Wolverine country to support one of their own. To understand Justin's appreciation, was evidenced as you watched him try to personally greet everyone there. Many of those in attendance were total strangers, yet Justin made every effort to thank everyone in the same way…with a loving hug. All the while, as he had done since first being diagnosed with his illness, he chose to ask questions about *their interests* and that which *they* loved to do. The man who told others of *"never giving up,"* was unselfish at every turn, regardless of his own personal, and emotional traumas.

In a touching, private ceremony on that same night, North Stafford Principal Thomas Nichols, along with Justin's counselor, Diana Smithey, donned their graduation robes, and honored him with his diploma. Justin waited for the large crowd attending the dinner and talent show to leave North Stafford, before his momentous graduation ceremony was to begin. Justin's family members, closest friends, other teachers, and coaches were standing proudly by his side. All Justin had wanted, was to be able to join his fellow graduates and receive his diploma. Because of his deteriorating health, most everything that was planned for Justin had to be moved forward. To see the snapshot of Justin's smiling face, complete with cap and gown, as he held his diploma across his chest was absolutely priceless. From the very beginning, members of the Whitaker family had been amazed at how many people came forward at critical times of need, and reached out their hands toward Justin at every turn. From classmates to total strangers, the crowds came in droves, as Justin's strength seemingly drew something out of them as well. One North Stafford student choosing to remain anonymous said, *"I never really knew Justin but learned about him from all my friends around me. When he died I felt so much pain, in ways that made me feel I had known him my whole life. It is so sad that our school lost our Superman, but now he can watch over us from the heavens."* Unfathomable grief, something so deeply emotional it was impossible to fully understand at the time, yet this loving sense of generosity continued on from fund raiser, to fund raiser. This truly was an aligned community helping one of their own. Justin himself was stunned at the large crowd during the talent show and dinner, and true to form all he could manage to say was that it *"made me feel great to know everyone cared. It gives me more strength inside."* Once again voicing quiet commentary, Justin Whitaker sought to thank others for simply caring for him. In reality, what he had done for an entire community offered all of *us* more strength, while sharply teaching us to focus on only things in life that are most important.

With Justin's death, I found myself far more altered in ways that made me feel as if I had lost my own son or daughter. That is the *gift* that Justin left within each and every one of us. That is why so many speak of him as an inspiration, and why people he never knew honored him at the time of his death, as tears filled their eyes. I have always told my children I love them each and every day, and they too, freely offer those same words in return. You are blessed with life but one day at a time, and assuredly, Justin Whitaker lived his life as an example for all of us. That is why you treasure those who love and care for you. So many have remarked that they think of Justin as an angel. I too have become one of those believers.

"I Felt Like Superman"

Each and every morning, like clockwork, I grab the remote and click on ESPN to catch my beloved 'Sports Center' show to get my fix of what went on in the world of sports the previous day and night. On the morning of June 24, 2008, at slightly past 6:30 a.m., I poured another cup of coffee as I prepped for work. Something told me to pause in the living room, and not tune out the next story. I sat down for a few minutes as the anchors introduced you to the story of John Challis, an eighteen year old baseball player from Freedom High School in Beaver County, Pennsylvania.

I have to say that since Justin's battle with cancer, and following his death in April, I have had these sporadic, emotional pangs within my heart. At a recent graduation party the weekend prior to the ESPN report on John Challis, I saw Craig Whitaker and took him aside. I wanted some time to pass as I prepared to write this book, before I told the Whitaker family of my plans in penning my thoughts honoring Justin's life, while mourning him in death. Yet on this night, there was another tug at my heart that urged me to tell him what my plans were. I told Craig I wanted to meet privately with the entire Whitaker family soon, so that I could gather more information about Justin's life and times. Craig was both appreciative, and stunned that I was about to take on this venture into both Justin's boyhood, and his tragic tale at life's end. I told Craig I was honored to be taking pen to paper for not only Justin, but in a way, for all those who suffered from such silent, deadly diseases. Again, as has been the case for some time, tears were shed, and we parted company with the plan to get together soon. I wish I could explain the motivations for all of this, yet they remain both truly personal, and often times, unexplainable to me. As was the case when speaking of the promise ring, and the tragedy surrounding the death of Kate McGloughan-Krzyzak, the story of John Challis literally sent chills up my spine.

ON THE SEVENTH DAY OF APRIL....SUPERMAN DIED

John Challis first learned that he had both liver, and lung cancer on June 23, 2006. Justin Whitaker battled his cancer for twenty two months, and like John, they both sported similar smiles, offered simple words of wisdom, and amazed those around them with their undying spirits, even as hope after hope was extinguished. John Challis' family had witnessed strengths in their son that consistently showed signs of immense courage, amidst a sense of maturity far beyond his young eighteen years of life. When he was asked one time where he managed to gain all of his wisdom from, John Challis matter-of-factly said, *"through cancer."* In many ways, the more I read about the life of John Challis, it became amazingly clear that Justin Whitaker had been cut from the same mold.

Justin and John also had true affection for their cherished baseball hats as well. Justin would jokingly spin his in any direction, depending on his mood and those around him. That would be, of course, if he wasn't patrolling an outfield sporting that dead-panned expression of competitive grit. Complete with eye black, it was *always* about fighting to win with Justin. John wore his Freedom cap proudly as well, with the brim curled like a pro player, and an inscription underneath that became his battle cry. *"Courage & Believe = Life."* Directly above this driven motto, was the name, *John Challis, #11.*

I perused numerous pieces by Pittsburgh Post-Gazette writer Mike White. Adjacent to several stories and blogs about John, were two videos shot by Matt Freed that captured my attention immediately. One was titled after John's motto of *'Courage & Believe = Life,'* and the other took my breath away, for it was named, *'I Felt Like Superman.'* Since commencing with my writings, it seemed that each time I sat down to think of my next section, I would come across information that hit me in a mystical, spiritual fashion. I am proud to say that in some way, the life and times of Justin Whitaker's life, somehow meshed into my own. Since his death, I don't think a day has gone by when yet another idea, subject, or thought about Justin has not entered my mind. The whole *'Superman'* subject arose once again with John Challis, akin to Justin having exceptionally strong bones when having bone marrow tests done (all the while mind you as he proudly wore his 'Superman' boxers). I hurriedly clicked on the 'Superman' video on the Post-Gazette site.

On April 14, 2008, exactly *seven* days following Justin's death, John Challis' Freedom High School team faced Aliquippa in baseball. There was barely 20-25 fans in attendance on this spring day, when Freedom head coach Steve Wetzel called on John Challis to pinch hit. Not too many people knew that John had not been in a batter's box for close to three years. At 5'5," and weighing about 95 pounds, John (wearing a protective jacket to cover his chest) glared out at the mound and took a cut at the first offering, a fastball down the middle. He wasted no time with bat to ball, and stung a single into right field. Very similar to Justin, when cancer had spread throughout his body and affected his legs as a result, he could barely run to first. He arrived at first base and was greeted by the base coach, who hugged John with tears streaming down his face. John screamed out, *"I did it. I did it,"* and all the players on both squads, proudly wearing the #11 on their hats, cheered this incredible moment. The Freedom team ran on the field to congratulate John, as his smile spread from ear to ear. This amazing moment was captured on video. How appropriate that this brief clip was entitled, *'I Felt Like Superman.'* As you watched this emotional clip, you couldn't help choking up as you heard John proclaim, *"I Felt Like Superman,"* when describing his feelings following the base hit. To watch this footage, was to shed tears for yet another baseball *'Superman,'* John Challis.

The similarities between the lives and times of two ball players, suffering from similarly painful, debilitating, dreadful cancers is uncanny. You feel the pains of two families, separated by close geographical boundaries, sharing undying love, and affection for their sons. Justin had passed from this earth, and right until the very end, he sought to hide his deepest pains and fears from those he loved, because he simply *"didn't want them to worry."* John Challis, following his heroic at bat, protected his mother from being interviewed just because he *"knew it would be too much for her to take."*

From Stafford County, Virginia, to Beaver County, Pennsylvania, you had two distinctively different communities treat each tragic story of two young men, with immeasurable dignity, and endless support. John shrugged his shoulders during one interview seen on video and remarked, *"why do people think it's so hard to see things the way I do? All I'm doing is making the best of a situation* (cancer). *Why can't people just see the best in things? It gets you so much further in life. It's always negative this, and negative that. That's all you see and hear. Life is not about how many breaths you take. It's what you do with those breaths that really counts."* John's strength mirrored Justin's in ways that would drop most people to their knees.

What John did not wish to dwell on, was the fact that in April of 2008, right after Justin had died, doctors had to inform the Challis family that his deadly cancer was spreading rapidly, and he had little time left. A walk-a-thon was organized by Freedom High's baseball coach Steve Wetzel, to raise money for a cruise for the Challis family. Knowing this would probably be his last vacation with his father Scott, his mother Regina, and his sister Alexis, after the walk-a-thon ended, John Challis stood and spoke to the crowd. Similar to the night of Justin's dinner and talent show in his honor, there was over 500 people present on the Freedom High School grounds. A hushed, saddened crowd listened to John as he said, *"I've got two options. I know I am going to die, so I can either sit home and feel sorry, or I could spread my message to everybody to live life to the fullest, and help those in need."* Most in attendance, wept at the crushing statement from this strong, courageous hero.

On June 5, 2008, John Challis fulfilled a promise he made to a school administrator from Freedom High School during his last hospital visit. He told him that *"I will graduate from high school,"* and John Challis, in cap and gown, did just that! Justin's hopes always hinged on graduating with the rest of the North Stafford senior class, yet it was just not in the cards for him. He was able to take happy memories with him though, as he *did* graduate from his beloved school, and those in support of him the entire way could not have been more proud. From story to story, Virginia to Pennsylvania, Justin Whitaker and John Challis shared amazing similarities and messages that *do* speak of inspiration and hope. Without ever knowing it, two eighteen year old boys taught so many about the true meanings of life.

On August 19, 2008, four months after Justin's death, John Challis died at his home, surrounded by loving family members. Sadly like Justin, John only had the chance to enjoy life for eighteen short years. Justin and John shared amazing parallels to one another in so many aspects of their lives. Both were diagnosed with cancer at sixteen, and both left indelible marks on everyone whose lives they touched every step of the way. Alex Rodriquez of the New York Yankees, had been advised of John's death as he prepared to play a game against the Toronto Blue Jays. John had spent an entire day with Alex in July, and was clearly emotionally distressed over John's passing. He was quoted on Major League Baseball's official site saying, *"he was a very brave boy with a huge heart. I was just proud that I got the chance to spend a whole day with him. It's something that I'll be inspired by for the rest of my life."* Rodriguez' comments mirrored those echoed by so many, not only about John Challis, but of Justin Whitaker as well. Pittsburgh Pirates President Frank Coonelly, released a statement to the press that said in part, *"John had every reason to complain about his situation, but he chose not to. What he did was show unfathomable courage, and great wisdom for someone so young. John's body could not win the battle with cancer, but John's tremendous spirit will live on amongst all those he, and his story impacted across the country."*

The Pirates first baseman, Adam LaRoche, was visibly upset when informed of John's death as he prepared to play a game against the St. Louis Cardinals. John had previously met LaRoche in June when he had the chance to spend a great day with Adam at PNC Park in Pittsburgh. After that time, LaRoche regularly talked to John on the phone, yet was told by the family that John did not have much time to live. In an interview with the Pittsburgh Post-Gazette following John's death, Adam said, *"It's depressing man. It makes you realize how short life is and how unfair it can be. But I think what's cool is that, even with what he had, he chose to make the best of it and touch a lot of lives that he wouldn't have, if this had not happened to him. He got the bad end of the deal, but he touched a lot of people. For sure, (motioning to his teammates in the Pirates locker room) he touched the twenty five people in here. He was special to me."* LaRoche remarked that he had invited John out to his Kansas ranch to hunt in the winter of 2008. Realizing now that John would not have that opportunity, LaRoche sadly said, *"I knew the chances weren't real good that he would make it and…it didn't work out. God had another plan for him."*

Look back and reflect on what Justin Whitaker's North Stafford baseball head coach, Jim Labrusciano said at his memorial service, when he emotionally told the audience that *"anytime his body aches, and he feels the need to complain, he simply closes his eyes and brings Justin Whitaker back."* John Challis had once voiced similar words. John was angry too regarding his illness, and at one point he began to cry and said, *"I'm not going to be able to have a son, get married, or have my own house. Those are the things I'm mad about…not dying."* There was again, an errie correlation between John Challis, and Justin Whitaker here as well. Because Justin's treatments were so intensive, even had he survived, he too would not have been able to father a child.

Justin Whitaker and Jon Challis…two ballplayers…two 'Supermen' whose courageous battles to live, reverberated loud enough for all of us to hear. As I reflect on their deaths, I am guessing that they have already met by now and said hello. They each still sport those famous grins that seemingly made your day a little lighter, when all the while in the last months of life, they suffered in dreadful pain. With gloves and a single baseball, I envision Justin and John playing light toss, laughing, and finally feeling pain free as they talked and threw the ball. We can let go now and feel the sanctity of their inner peace.

When Your Boy Was a Baby

When driving back from a baseball tournament, I paused to steal a glance.

My son, fourteen now, was readying to take the turn into high school.

Eighth grade was seemingly in the rear view mirror, yet where did the time go?

I let my mind flash back to times, when at night, Nick would sleep on my chest.

The peaceful tranquility of your child at rest, never shall I forget the peace it offered.

Watching him run through the house with only a diaper on, a smile upon his face.

Today he strides through the house, shorts, no shirt, cut lean and chiseled.

He stands eye to eye with me now, truly a man-child about to blossom.

I am proud of this fine young man, for he is a son that has forever made me smile.

We forever strive in seeking the best for our own, often times at the expense of ourselves.

I have found myself reflecting more recently about my own closure in coaching him.

Since t-ball and instructional football, long before an adolescent swagger appeared,

I had been a mentor and disciplinarian in all of his sports...the coach and kid evolving.

Cruelly, I told him that at times, I may have to bark a little louder, use him as an example.

Never seeking to show favoritism...never having others believe he was the coach's kid,

Nick would look up with his big brown eyes and say, "I understand Dad."simple words.

Year after year as parents, we take new snapshots and add them to our endless collection.

In one photo he holds a miniscule bat, while in another, he barely can hold a football.

Through it all you witness growth and a gaining of stability, as a child seeks his footing.

My daughter Alyssa, approaching teen land, leaves me amazed and startled at times.

Equally tall and lean, a gifted student athlete in her own right…my blue eyed cutie.

God knows that when the day arrives for her entry into high school, I will feel the same.

Common sense says that seeing your little girl emerge becomes more traumatic…sad.

I do believe there is truth in that, for even now, I am more protective of her than ever.

When this last baseball season arrived, I vowed that I would coach, while also watch.

At fourteen years old, skills you taught, regardless of the sport, have been ingrained.

Committed to memory after hundreds of hours of work, you can only say, "do your best."

As Nick prepared for his county track championships, I drifted away…day dreamed.

Remembering how I too, had taken to track, yet equally recalled having no audience.

Regardless how hectic and busy our lives may be, you never get a second chance at this.

And so it is in what in all likelihood is this final season, as Dad and son bid adieu.

I can honestly say that I would have it no other way, for I tried my best to lead him here.

It is his place now, his time to plant his feet and display what he has learned in sports.

And I shall sit back in pride at the accolades he receives, hoping that I made a difference.

Two weeks ago at a local meet, I was stunned at how sleek and fast Nick had become.

After his final dash in a leg of the relay, I watched in amazement while he sprinted.

Later, before he boarded the bus, he walked over, shook my hand, and hugged me.

As I walked away, I had flashbacks of precious years gone by far too quickly.

In my own selfish way, he was still a baby sleeping on my chest again…my loving son.

That writing, *When Your Boy Was A Baby,'* was a passage written about my son Nicholas over five years ago, when he and Justin were still competing in AAU baseball together. Nick, Justin, and all of the boys were closing out the eighth grade, with the knowledge that in all likelihood, most would never play together on the same team again. As we drove back from Maryland on that day, I watched as Nick was drifting off to sleep after a weekend of games, and you could not help but to visit memory lane and remember the beginnings of it all. We all do that as parents.

The innocence of a child, cascading memories of occasions laced between restful peace, and utter chaos. From still photo images of a baby's first crawl, to those precious first steps, infancy aimlessly weaves into adolescence at the blink of an eye. Fatherly pride emerges as Dad's boy becomes a young man. A child whispers "Dad" in your ear, and suddenly life's responsibilities arise, and serves as a challenge to everything you are as a person. This living, breathing individual, placing his tiny hand inside your own as you walk down a street, offers warmth, and a sense of happiness that prior to this moment, you had never known before. Even now, in dream-like tranquility, I drift back in time to my own youthful years. Throughout my own adolescence, most adult men

ON THE SEVENTH DAY OF APRIL....SUPERMAN DIED

I ever encountered way back when, were forever protective of the messages within their hearts.

A baby's incoherent mumblings transforms into broken words, and once again a man is further captured by this tiny creature learning to communicate in his own special way. Months soon become years, and the days of rockers, cradles, and high chairs turn to preschool and beyond. You are now witness to the fully charged mind of a miniature man, yearning to understand life (yes...all of it) through question, upon endless question. When a child is three or four years old, questions are fired upon parents with an unrelenting bombardment of emotion. God bless the children for their inquiries, for they seem to allow all of us a mode for backtracking our own travels through time as little people. It's funny how even today, your own world, filled with decision making quandaries, often times returns us to the memories of our past, and the teachers who once served as our guides toward the future. My early life instructors, Mom and Dad, have long since passed from this life. I believe that in order to seek out answers to the underlying meanings within our adult lives, we must reflect on the innocence of our own childhood days, and the vast messages learned along the way. I think in ways, that is why tragedies such as Justin's death, makes us all keenly aware that what you may have today, *can* vanish tomorrow. You value all of the good things in your life, and the love in your heart, and for those reasons, never let a day pass when you fail to tell your children that you love them. You watch your child grow day by day, and you keep your fingers crossed that they remain clear from harm's way. The sad part is, all journeys are not the same, and we should all count our blessings for each precious day shared with those we love.

As much as we may complain about the years of travel sports, I honestly don't think our lives would have been so enriched if we missed this journey. I close my eyes often, and remember the road trips and AAU tournament games, and count my blessings that Nick will now move on into college, and that his travels will be safe and full of life's experiences. My daughter continues on in field hockey, and soccer at sixteen now, and I know that one day soon, I will again be saddened when reflecting on the passage of time. I also close my eyes and see Justin waving that bat on many a road trip, or smiling at you in a way that always seemed to capture his innocence. His vibrant, youthful bounce when he walked, made you stop and smile too. I am pained that like Nick, Courtney, and all of their friends, that Justin is not moving forward on a collegiate path. I am sure that if he were, all those touched by Justin's heart and soul in college, would have shared the same affection, and admiration we had for him in such a brief time here. He just had that way about him.

Since April 7, 2008 when Justin Whitaker passed away, I have tried to take a little bit of precious 'me' time to jot thoughts down, all in an effort to grasp that which is most valued in life, and gain some sense of rational perspective. Life *is* about life and death, trials and tribulations, and yes…victories, and defeats. It does not always entail sports, nor should it, because the worlds in which we live in on a day to day basis, are far more complex, and vastly different for each and every one of us. For someone like Justin Whitaker, he merely got a taste of the joys of life and love, before his courageous battle ended after a minute stay on this fine earth. He was that same little baby you brought home from the hospital. He played hard as a little boy, dirtied his hands and knees, and repeated the same drill day after day, as he played in neighborhoods, and on fields during steaming, hot summer days. Over time, Justin gave those he loved beautiful memories, images forever captured within our minds, and photographs that will never fade from view.

How one child is blessed with survival, and another is mourned in death, is a topic that will never be known as time passes us by here. That truly has been a matter that has bothered me for a lifetime, when I am troubled and pained over someone that passed far before their time. Maybe one fine day, we will *all* have the answers that so plague our hearts after years of loss and anguish. We all miss those 'noises' from a busy house, as we watched our children grow into adults. Every once in a while, sit in your favorite chair, and glance at a hallway that once had a child racing around a corner, stopping our own hearts as they flew by with reckless abandon. Then lean back and close your eyes, and if you let yourself go…if you try hard enough, you *can* almost smell the skin of a newborn child, as they paused in their busy day, and slept on your chest a while.

Sweet memories of days gone by. Never will they be forgotten.

When Athletes Are Not Just in It for Sports

I have played different sports my whole life, and later I decided to coach, *not* because I had a child playing. It was far deeper than that. Go to any athletic complex anywhere in this country, whether it is an indoor or outdoor event, and you see the true essence of what sports are all about. From t-ball, to instructional levels, we watch games as parents and we all harbor hopeful thoughts that our young athlete turns out to be someone special. We know in our hearts how much we love our kids, yet a different kind of animal often emerges when our children's teams lock horns with an enemy squad.

Justin's North Stafford High School, has fierce rivals within their Commonwealth District seasons, regardless of the sport played. Whether true "enemy" teams emerged through a single event that stoked the flames of competition, or have been around for years, like every division in the land, rivals clash and stories are added to history books. My son Nick, and daughter Alyssa, have competed against North Stafford teams in many different sports, and tight geographical boundaries naturally make them a pre-determined enemy I suppose. As discussed earlier, an amazing thing happened around Stafford County sports fields, when the word spread that Justin's illness had worsened, and his physical condition significantly weakened.

Because of the fact that Justin's baseball friends lived in different areas of the county, most of those who shared the same AAU uniforms when growing up with him during travel leagues, drifted to high schools other than North Stafford. Justin actually started school at Colonial Forge for a semester his freshman year, and then transferred to North Stafford. He went from a brief stint as an Eagle, transitioned to a Wolverine, and he never looked back. The friends he left behind at Forge remained as true, loyal companions. Justin's friends *always* remained as Justin's friends.

ON THE SEVENTH DAY OF APRIL....SUPERMAN DIED

I recall going to a football game to watch my son compete in for Colonial Forge, and as I walked through the gate and toward the stands, there was Justin standing there, always surrounded by friends. Since I had been an assistant coach on his AAU squad, Justin has always held a special place in my heart. Maybe it was because in him, I actually saw visions of myself when playing sports. At times, I was that same 'Energizer Bunny,' full throttle always, and never slowing down to wait for the rest of my body to catch up. He had that same tenacity that grips many driven athletes seeking to succeed in sports, never wanting to disappoint anyone. When I remarked earlier about watching Justin standing in a batter's box in that grip and rip pose, I can relate to that picture and understand his grit and determination, because that was *me*. Justin was unduly hard on himself if he failed to hit the baseball, struck out, or felt that in some small part, he had let his team down. There was never a grey area with him, and I shared that same passion. On that crisp, fall football eve as I approached the fence line, Justin turned and made eye contact with me. He had lost most of his hair, and I suppose to some, he may not have looked like the Justin they used to know. But to me, those eyes that lit up never faded, as he turned, and whatever conversation he was having with friends stopped for a few minutes. He walked over to me, and as always, gave me that sports hug that we all know and cherish. In those few seconds, all he said was *"hey Mr. Lanciault, how are you doing?"* I will admit, and those closest to me can readily attest, that there are times in my life when sensitivities creep in, and I feel raw emotion wash over me when it is least expected. Throughout my law enforcement career, the myriad of sad cases I have dealt with may have contributed to that. Yet, this moment was vastly different. As I hugged Justin and asked him how he was, I remember walking away in disbelief that he wondered how *I* was doing. We all know through his family, and words spoken by his girlfriend Courtney, that this *was* Justin at every turn. I can pause right now and take in that moment in time as if it were yesterday. It's funny how we bring bits of time back to us, whether our memories are good or bad. Even now that wave of sadness hits me, and I have to pause and reconcile the fact that a wonderful boy, and solid baseball player has passed from this earth. In that wake, Justin Whitaker left a void behind for all of us to deal with.

There was well over 2,000 people in attendance at North Stafford High School on the day of his memorial service, and I would venture to say that well over half, if not more, were kids from all over the county. While sitting below, I saw coaches from every team in the stands, as opposing players in suits and ties stared aimlessly toward Justin's casket. One Commonwealth District opponent squad, Massaponax High School, caught the full attention of all in attendance. Every player wore their baseball hats with a dominant letter 'M' on the front, as a tribute to the fallen Wolverine. To me, it was an honorable sign of respect given to a fellow baseball player...an athlete who so loved his game.

When your eyes moved forward to the front, it was only fitting that Justin's casket was blue, with flower arrangements in blue and orange, the famed colors of the North Stafford Wolverines. Baseball surrounded Justin even in death, as one touching array of flowers, had the number '7' in its center. The one that made you feel pain later was a beautiful heart shaped arrangement of roses, with two baseballs in the middle. Family members told me later that one was for Justin, and the other for Courtney. I mentioned at the beginning how the gymnasium was so still and solemn, and during the slide show presentation honoring Justin's life, you could hear people sobbing as image upon image flashed by. I suppose this is when we all had our senses of reality slapped back into us. At first we could not fathom that 'Superman' had actually left us, until we arrived here to this moving memorial service. For me, to see all the teams present, and to see the pain in everyone's eyes over this tragic loss, placed everything into somber perspective.

There were other stories tied to athletes memorializing Justin Whitaker unselfishly. Courtney Crews decided to play softball in college for Hofstra University, and when she signed her letter of intent, none other than Justin Whitaker stood proudly by her side. Long before Courtney would arrive to play for the school, other members of the Hofstra squad heard about Justin's illness, and wanted to let another soon-to-be teammate know that they cared for, and supported her. The girls ordered black shirts with the words, "Join the Fight" on the back.

ON THE SEVENTH DAY OF APRIL....SUPERMAN DIED

The amazing thing to Courtney, was that some of the players contacted Courtney, and remarked that even after meeting Justin only one time, they said that he had made indelible impacts on their lives. Anyone knowing Justin at all, even for a brief span of time, often came away saying the same thing.

Shortly after Justin's burial, I went to my son's Colonial Forge baseball game at home against North Stafford. While talking with parents, I saw Justin's father Craig walk toward me, and like always, we hugged and said hello. I glanced to my right and also saw Courtney, the star catcher for the Wolverines softball team. She was greeting kids from many different schools, and as always, had that smile that made you feel at ease in seconds. The game was a big Commonwealth battle, and as I glanced out toward the Colonial Forge bench area, I watched in amazement as once again, an alleged "enemy" team honored Justin Whitaker. The Forge squad all wore black warm-up jerseys with the number '7' on the back, and the letters 'JW' on the chest. The 'JW' initials were in the location where Justin normally wore his Superman logo. I believe it was the first time Justin's dad had seen the shirts, and you could tell he was emotionally moved by the Forge team's gesture. Most of the Colonial Forge squad, including my son, had played on either the Stafford Hurricanes, or Virginia Thunder AAU teams together before high school. It was just the *"right thing to do,"* according to most of the Forge athletes. That is how you honored a teammate. Nathan Moore, a Wolverine baseball player, would later say that Justin was a *"gift to us all."* That was most assuredly an understatement.

Two days after Justin's death, the North Stafford baseball team squared off against a gritty Albemarle team. Lead by star pitcher Zack Miller's thirteen strikeouts, the Wolverines handily beat Albemarle 8-4. There was, however, one more important thing to do before they left the field on this day. Nate Moore walked over to Craig Whitaker and gave him a signed game ball, and hugged him as the Wolverines again...celebrated with Justin. All the players took turns coming over to hug Craig with the number seven, stitched to the side of their ball caps. The mission that day by the Wolverines, valiantly struggling with their own saddened emotions, was to win this first game back *"for Justin."* His

#7 shirt hung on the dugout fence as a reminder of what they needed to do. Craig was clearly moved by Justin's entire team fighting through their own pains, and honoring him this way. Craig said to me numerous times since Justin's death, that some days are more difficult than others, and this heaviness of sadness remains but that he was just *"proud to be given the opportunity to be his father. His love brought a community closer together. That is the true essence of Justin."*

Courtney's love for Justin never went unnoticed by anyone, at any time. Sports had always been a great part of her life too, and for the most part, Justin was there to support her as much as she did him. In her first game back playing softball against Albemarle, Courtney, who had always been a pillar of strength during Justin's arduous fight against cancer, struggled to maintain her composure. She walked out to the batter's box as the starting catcher, and struggled mightily as she held back tears, gulping for air. Courtney, in Justin-like fashion, wiped tears away, pulled on her mask, and settled behind home plate. Each time Courtney took the field between innings, she slapped a wooden board that hung on the chain link fence with the initials of 'DIFJW' (*'Do It For Justin Whitaker'*). During the first couple innings, she glanced into the North Stafford stands, almost in an effort to see her loving companion rooting her on as he always did. Justin was not there, yet the number '7' was seen on shirts of fans, and across balloons waving in the spring breeze. The Wolverine girls also had green ribbons attached to their uniforms, with the number '7' proudly in the center.

When I sat down with Courtney, she recalled that even before her softball game started, one day after Justin died, she *knew* he was there. In what can only be described as mystifying, her Wolverine teammates scored 7 runs in the first inning. There was an eerie feeling on the bench realizing what that '7' on the scoreboard meant. The softball team went on to win 9-0. With the baseball team winning their game 8-4, Courtney related to me that she and her friends sat down and were stunned at something. Call it a play of mere numbers, or wish it as some form of divine message, but they looked at the numbers, and could not believe what they saw. Taking all the numbers, inclusive of the 7 runs scored by the ladies in the first inning, you have two sets of dates that made everyone sit back and have an "oh my God" moment. One set is 9-7-89, which coincided with Justin's birth date. The other set was 4-7-08, which signified the date of his passing. Some may say that numbers can be bent and turned to fit most any occasion, drafting meanings to them, yet I believe that these numbers between two North Stafford athletic teams on the same day, *were* worthy of attention. Courtney said that when the game started she glanced into the stands, wishing that number seven was there watching. Quite possibly that '7' that flashed onto the scoreboard in the first inning was a very good sign that he was.

As Courtney finished explaining of the games and number oddities, Craig said that over and over again, there were all sorts of signs that Justin and his presence, remained for us to take notice of. Shortly after Justin had passed away, Craig and his son Jordie decided to take a trip down to Virginia Beach, VA. They wanted to see the spot on the pier where Justin had given Courtney her promise ring. They went to the spot and felt in touch with the 'Promise Ring' moment that happened a couple months prior. A thunderstorm was about to hit and they ran into the hotel. As the storm hit and the rain fell hard outside, Craig walked out to the balcony and looked over the edge. He could not believe what he saw. There was nobody else on the boardwalk, with the exception of a young man with his shirt off. As Craig leaned over, he noticed that as the man stood at the rail, he had a black, number seven on the center of his back. He called out to Jordie who saw it as well, and Craig said he simply could not believe it. There was no sense to it at all, because the heavy rains had forced everyone else into their hotels.

Craig credited the Free Lance Star, and Washington Post newspapers, as instrumental to all the support his family received during such a long, difficult ordeal. *"The newspapers honored Justice in ways that we can never thank them enough for. Their work allowed everyone to feel Justin, and strangers came to understand the essence of who he was, and how hard he fought."*

What most outsiders never knew, is that Justin made Courtney promise at one point, *never* to miss a softball game, or anything else in her life for that matter, because of his illness. This was an eighteen year old girl who slept but a few hours at night, between hospital visits, and setting up fundraisers for Justin's medical expenses. That did not include all of her responsibilities as the President of the North Stafford Student Council Association. Athletically, she managed to rise from sleep at 4 a.m. on most days, so that she did not miss sessions with her trainer readying her for softball. When Justin became very ill following his bone marrow transplant, Courtney watched him ache from painful sores in his mouth and extremities, losing both his appetite, and his hair. Most people her age would have been too withered, and shaken to be of any assistance and support. Courtney stood strong, and even injected medicine through a tube in Justin's chest, then would later flush it clean. Whenever she made trips to the doctor with Justin, she would sneak up on the examining table, and snuggle close to him, always letting him know she was there. Courtney believed that she was able to gain her strength to persevere through such hard times, because of how Justin chose to valiantly battle his illness. She watched for close to two years as Justin somehow managed to maintain a positive attitude, regardless of the dire circumstances surrounding him on a daily basis.

The Washington Post would later interview her leadership teacher, Leigh Swift, who shed some light on the type of person Courtney Crews is. Ms. Swift was amazed that *"sometimes when she's in my class, I'll look at her, and I can't even imagine what's going through her head. It's so much for a high school senior to think about."* This was *not* your average high school senior...not even close.

To understand the strength in Courtney Crews, was to see how the events of April 7, 2008 unfolded. Justin had been taken off life support at about 2 p.m. The family was amazed as two hours passed, yet Justin sustained life...the batter in the box never giving up. Justin hung on for close to two more hours battling. Courtney left Inova, and was driving home, because as she told me, *"she could not bear to watch Justin take his last breath."* Just as she was pulling into her driveway, Courtney received a call from her dad who told her that Justin had passed away. A crowd of over 600 people were already gathering on the grounds of North Stafford High School for a candlelight vigil, after word of Justin's death spread through the county. It was now close to 6:30 p.m., and one would think that a grieving girlfriend, who had stood by Justin's side through every turn of his dreadful illness, would have succumbed to sheer exhaustion. Ever the vigilant companion, Courtney *knew* where she had to be. She went to the high school, *their* high school, and most were shocked that she held the strength to attend the vigil. You could have heard a pin drop when the mournful audience watched Courtney, donning her NSHS jacket, take the microphone and speak. It was clear that Justin's valiant demeanor through the worst of times, had now spread through a simple message that Courtney *had* to deliver. Amidst complete silence, Courtney said, *"I know we're all sad, but the last thing Justin wants to do is look down and see all of us in tears."* Tears flowed freely, and emotions that had been kept in check to this point, escaped most in attendance. Courtney later told media members present that she had been strong because of all of the support from family and friends surrounding her, but she *"couldn't figure out how I'm able to move on from here, without him by my side."* When I met with Courtney a couple months later, I asked if she had any regrets or feelings she had yet to share. All she mentioned was that on Monday when Justin had passed away, *"I wish I had stayed later, and on that next day, I wish I had not gone to school or played in that game. But Justin would get angry if any games were missed by anyone because of his illness, and my games were no exception. He wanted me to play right until the end, just like he always did."*

For the better part of twenty two months, Courtney had been a loyal, dedicated companion for someone she loved, and nothing in her world held a higher precedence than that. I spoke to Justin's father Craig on many an occasion at baseball diamonds, and at graduation parties over the summer, and each and every time, he spoke of his love for Courtney, and how she was like a *"daughter to me. I will do everything I can for her forever."*

As a parent of a senior, I believe that regardless of this rite of passage, you *do* feel emotions of unrest and anxiety, knowing that your child is soon leaving home. For Courtney and her senior year, it pained me to know that while others held fond memories of their senior proms, and were loading scrapbooks with pictures of all that they had enjoyed in high school, Courtney still had a mountain to climb. The boy she had come to like as a child, and love as a young man, would no longer be by her side as they embarked on college careers and beyond. The lives of Justin and Courtney at North Stafford High School, are memories locked away now, yet never a moment shared forgotten. As in the last out of a game,

Courtney could now stand up, remove her catcher's mask, and be proud that she is the person that she is. Many have said that Courtney is far outside the realm of what a *normal* high school teenager stands for. That alone, gave Justin every reason on this earth, to fight the fight that he did, as if the game had *never* ended. Courtney Crews offered that same mirror image.

The day following Justin's death, she walked off the softball field and had to go to the baseball field. She was tired, dirty, and emotionally spent. She was seen talking with close friends, exchanging hugs, and tears were a common theme as a school and county mourned. At one final point on this early eve, she was standing completely alone and stared into the North Stafford dugout. In one darkened corner, a single, North Stafford baseball uniform shirt, Justin's #7, blew aimlessly in the breeze. He was there all the time. Courtney always knew he would be there for her.

Two days before Courtney would depart for Hofstra University in New York to begin college and softball, we met at a coffee shop to talk once again. I felt that it was important for her to privately speak to me, without others present, so that she could have her time. Throughout the year and nine months of Justin's illness, Courtney had been a vigilant, loving, supporting best friend to Justin Whitaker. She never wavered, regardless of the calamity and chaos surrounding her, and the Whitaker family at every turn. So many have spoken of her strength and vibrant drive. I too, was a witness to that.

I asked Courtney how she was feeling about everything, as almost five months had passed since Justin's death. Courtney said, *"I still find it almost unreal to accept. Even now when I go out with friends, as we end an evening, I find myself wanting to call Justin just to talk. There have been so many times when I absentmindedly hit his name in my directory, then I am snapped back to reality. It just seems so wrong and unreal, even now. As I am preparing now to go to college, I think about how Justin never went there with me, and how I wanted him to see it just to get a feel for where I would be and that I would be safe. I know that the first couple weeks of September will be especially hard. September seventh was Justin's birthday, and September tenth would have been our fourth anniversary as a couple together. I think the seventh will be really hard because it falls on a Sunday, and because of what that number means anyway. The tenth may not be as bad because*

ON THE SEVENTH DAY OF APRIL....SUPERMAN DIED

I will be in class, my training, and probably practicing later. I think staying busy will keep my mind free of sadness."

 Courtney and I talked about many things not related to Justin's passing. Each time we did talk, it was always amazing to me that she was only eighteen years old. She had a way about her, that made you feel as if she had everything under control, and was on top of it all. I knew that she would still have days that would mire her in sadness, yet that is because of the way she cared for, and loved Justin. It was just her way. As we talked about Justin's gravesite, Courtney told me that for the first couple months after his passing, she would go there at least three to four times a week. She would not stay long, but would say her peace, talk a bit, and go home. Many nights she chose to drive to North Stafford's baseball field and hang out there a while. She knew this was Justin's safe haven, and felt calm and happy knowing the happiness Justin experienced there. Courtney said, *"on April seventh when Justin died, I knew that this had to be the first place I needed to be. Even when I had games on the softball field, I found myself always glancing toward the baseball field. It was just our place. A lot of people probably never knew how close Justin and I really were. When I lost him, I lost a major piece of my heart. I know it will be a long while before the pain I am feeling now will fade. I think about playing my first college softball game, knowing that Justin won't be there. I suppose I wonder too, how I will feel if someone else asks me out for a date. I have all these things run through my mind, and pain creeps in again. Since Justin died, even when I go out with friends, things are different. It just feels odd and out of place...depressing. I think differently now. I used to worry about small problems, or heard of small issues with kids at school, and they magnified how much it affected their lives. I learned through Justin how life itself means far more than tiny, insignificant things. I know it will take quite a bit of time to be myself again."*

 On a beautiful, hot August day, Courtney and I exchanged a few laughs too, as she reflected on the happy times with Justin at his house. Courtney said, *"the first time I drove over to his house after he died, I just expected him to be there. It seemed so strange not to have him pop out of the house, or be inside waiting for me. I walked into his room and it suddenly hit me that it was the very last place we were in, before he got really sick again. We made some popcorn and watched a movie. I have such great memories of his house, and all the special moments* shared with him. It's funny but my emotions are sometimes so very different from time to time. When Justin was first diagnosed with cancer, or things in his treatment went badly, I was so angry. I was so mad that he was taken from me, and from his family. For a long time my anger was intense. Then I remembered how much pain he was in all the time, and I took comfort in the fact that he was no longer in agony. For the most part, knowing that he is in a better place now makes me feel so much better."

A few times as we talked, I could hear Courtney's voice change to another level, and noticed tears slightly welling up in her eyes. This competitive, hard charging athlete had another side to her too. I could feel her anguish as we talked, and varied nerves were struck that brought her back in time. I certainly did not wish to conjure up bad memories, yet in a way, she seemed at ease in this private setting as a way to release some inner emotions. Our talk moved into Virginia Beach, and Justin giving her the promise ring. Courtney began to lay out the whole weekend as if it was yesterday. She said, *"I left for Virginia Beach on a Thursday because of my softball tournament. Justin was going to come down on a Saturday with my parents. Justin had told me that Friday was spent all day at the hospital gearing up for the trip, just to make sure he could make it. He said that his white blood cell and platelet counts were way down. He told me that he had to be infused with two bags of platelets just to make the trip. That Saturday, the weather turned pretty chilly. Justin had a sweatshirt on, with his letterman's jacket. He was also wrapped in a blanket because he had to keep his body warm. That night we all went out to eat at Rockefeller's restaurant, and it was about 8:30 p.m. when Justin and I walked out together on the pier, and then onto a stretch of beach. Justin was acting really nervous and I knew something was up. I saw my mother hand him something, but still didn't know what was going on. Justin was so cute. He said, "you know how much I love you. I want to spend the rest of my life with you, and I promise to love you forever. Do you feel the same?" At first, I said no! Justin had this semi-shocked look on his face, before I quickly said yes as he gave me the promise ring. It was very special. We stayed half of that Sunday, had breakfast, hit some stores, and then grabbed some ice cream. March 23rd is my birthday, so we celebrated it with the ice cream. "*

I felt immediate sadness as we paused for a few minutes, and talked about how quickly Justin became very sick as soon as they returned home from Virginia Beach. Courtney said, *"Craig told me that Justin got very sick, was home, and rather out of it. It's funny but as he became sick, I remembered how*

ON THE SEVENTH DAY OF APRIL...SUPERMAN DIED

Justin and I talked about the possibility of him not beating this cancer and dying. During really rough times when the chemo was not working, or after the bone marrow transplant failed, Justin would say, "maybe it would be easier on you if I died." But, he also knew me and said right after that, "but you never give up Courtney, so how can I?" There were times he would even bring up the subject of us breaking up, just so I didn't have to go through all of this with him. All I would say is, Justin Whitaker, are you insane? I wouldn't even listen to him."

On April 1st, at about 8:30 a.m., Courtney received a phone call from her mother, telling her that Justin spiked a high temperature of 103 and had to be taken to Mary Washington Hospital in Fredericksburg to be stabilized. Justin would later be taken to Inova Fairfax Hospital after that. Courtney explained that *"right after my game on Tuesday, my dad was going to drive me up to the hospital, but Justin was heavily medicated and it made no sense. At about 1:30 a.m., on Wednesday, Craig called me and said that Justin had suffered seizures. We all went to the hospital and stayed with him until about 4:30 or 5:00 a.m. Craig and I had a very emotional talk then. He said to me, "Courtney, he's dying. We're losing him. You are losing your best friend...your boyfriend." I'm thinking to myself, Craig had made the decision with Shelia to turn life support off, and they are losing* **their son.** *When Craig first told me Justin was dying, I was so shocked. I didn't want him to give up, and Justin always beat everything before, so why not this? I knew that I didn't want to cry in Justin's room. The doctor had said before this that Justin was medicated but would be able to hear people talking. I didn't want him to hear me crying. I stepped out with my dad and got so angry. I told my father how wrong this was, and that Justin did not deserve this. I was probably in a state of shock I guess, with all of that happening at once."*

Once Courtney knew that Justin's fight may soon be over, she took it on herself to seek out Zac right away, knowing that a best friend needed to know where the situation stood at the time. There was an event at North Stafford, and Courtney found out Zac was there. Courtney explained that moment further. She said, *"I walked up to Zac, and he probably knew by my face that I had some type of bad news. I took him aside and told him exactly what Craig said, that Justin was dying. I just looked at him and said that he was not going to make it. I think we were both in a state of shock. I couldn't hold it in with Zac and was crying. He tried to be strong as we hugged each other and talked privately for about ten minutes. Zac is a very strong guy. I know* how hard it has been for him watching Justin slip away, but I know that in time he will be o.k. There were so many teachers, coaches, and especially senior students who offered so much support in those final days."

During this private talk with Courtney, I knew that inevitably, we would talk about the final day of April 7th, as family and friends gathered near Justin's bedside in the ICU. Courtney said, *"when Craig and Shelia made the decision to remove life support from Justin, it hit everyone so hard. Up until this moment, it just didn't seem real. I think everyone was there at about 12:30 or 1:00 p.m. I believe it was closer to 2:00 p.m., when the machine was shut down. Justin fought and stayed alive for close to three hours. I couldn't bear to watch him take his last breath, and about forty five minutes, to an hour before he died, I kissed him and told him I loved him. I told my dad I could not stay, and to call me when he had passed away. I drove home and don't even remember the ride. Just as I pulled into my driveway, my father called and said that Justin had died. I told my brother Trevor that Justin had died, and then walked into my room and cried alone for about five or ten minutes. Trevor was very close to Justin, and we comforted each other for a while. A candlelight vigil for Justin was set for 6:00 p.m., and I knew that North Stafford High School was where I needed to be. I had to get there too, to speak to Coach Labrusciano and tell him personally that Justin had passed away. I was sure he probably knew, but it was personal with me. A bunch of my friends picked me up and took me to the field. Coach Labrusciano was at the baseball field, and I met him and we walked into center field. I told him that Justin had passed away, and we talked for close to twenty minutes. He was incredibly helpful and supportive telling me that Justin was in a far better place now, and that I had to take care of myself. He took it very, very hard too. I then walked over to the seniors and talked to all of them, who took it just as hard. Maybe it was because we all knew that Justin had taken a bad turn and were prepared for this, but nobody cried. We all hugged each other and it was very quiet, almost peaceful."*

Courtney told me that she was absolutely stunned at how many people had already gathered at North Stafford, after word spread throughout the county about Justin's death. Courtney added, *"I knew that Justin was very popular, and so many people supported him at every turn, but I was blown away by the people at the vigil. There were kids there from just about every Commonwealth District team, and so many of them were so emotionally upset and crying. It was then that I knew I wanted to speak to everyone. I don't remember exactly what I said, but it was something to the effect of knowing that it was a very rough day and that everyone was sad. I mentioned that Justin would want us to have a few laughs too, and I think I even made a couple jokes just so everyone could wipe their tears away, and smile a bit. Everyone was crushed with sadness. I was too, but I wanted them to know that Justin was at peace now."*

As we neared the end of our talk, Courtney mentioned to me that she had worries about Craig, Jordie, Shelia, and Amber. As she was about to embark on her collegiate career, she was deeply troubled about the days ahead for everyone. Courtney said, *"I look at Craig and as we talk, he is so unselfish that he actually says he feels sorry for me because Justin has died. I think to myself, my God, he had to make a decision to remove his son from life support, plan a funeral, and worry about Jordie, and his emotional issues all at once. His strength amazed me always. With Jordie, I always remember how he and Justin got into those typical brotherly fights, but I also know just how much Justin meant to him, and how hard it is for Jordie to move on in life without him. He looked up to Justin in ways that sometimes nobody saw. Justin always cared for, and protected Jordie when he was younger. I vowed to Justin that I would always continue to do the same, and treat him as if he were my little brother. As for Shelia and Amber, they are grieving over the loss of Justin in the same ways. They miss him so much. I remember how on some nights, Justin and I would be hanging out and Shelia would stop by, and we would do something together. Justin and his mom had a very special, loving bond. When Justin was very sick, Shelia like Craig, would stay at the hospital so that he was never alone. Justin shared that same bond with Amber. I can't leave out Justin's grandparents, Barbara and Darrell, either. There has been so much pain, and now we need to remember Justin for the person that he was."*

Minutes from saying goodbye, Courtney and I talked lightly about her future plans, and the world in front of her as she readied for college at Hofstra. Courtney said, *"I always talked to Zac about maybe one day owning my own indoor and outdoor sports complex. I have an interest in Sports Marketing as my major, and just felt like the whole sports thing would make for an ideal living. But, I wouldn't mind playing on the United States national softball team either!"* We shared a good laugh, and for the first time since we talked, Courtney Crews was able to show me a full smile.

As we finished our drinks, I asked Courtney how being side by side with Justin during his illness, and ultimately watching as he slipped away, had altered her life. She paused for a few seconds and quietly said, *"I feel more grown up now, more mature I guess. I think throughout all of this, I will be able to handle any adversities that come my way a lot better. So many people have talked about my strength, saying that they don't think that if they were in my shoes, that they could be so strong. I never felt I was anything out of the ordinary. I loved Justin as my best friend. I think when faced with a similar tragedy, we would all be able to reach down and do the same things. If I have taken anything from all of this, it would be that nobody should ever take anything in life for granted. Whether it is in friendships, or relationships, you need to really look at each and every situation, especially for those you love and care about. You just never know how much time you have to spend with those closest to you. Justin made me understand all of that."*

As we walked to our vehicles, I wished Courtney the best of luck at school. We hugged and said goodbye. It was the kind of hug that made you feel the heart and soul of a courageous person. I have spoken to so many people, in all walks of life, who always commented about the way Justin Whitaker had made an impact on their lives, as he valiantly fought cancer. Courtney Crews too, took every punch along the way, and never once, did she seek pity. She was merely fighting the fight, just as Justin did for close to two years…soul mates.

A Brother and Sister…Grandparents Grieving

When preparing to discuss Justin's brother Jordan, better known as Jordie by most, and the effect that Justin's death had on him, I realized at the very beginning that it would be a very tender time for the family. I knew that the pains felt by Justin's mom Shelia, as well as by Justin's sister Amber, were no less emotional.

Jordie had turned seventeen by the time of this writing, and one day Craig told me with tear filled eyes, that Jordie had taken Justin's death very, very hard. I remember Jordie when coaching AAU baseball, and seeing him at varied tournaments. He was always very much to himself and quiet for the most part. Then again, I was comparing him to Justin, the class clown, always with the smile and energy galore. Craig said that since Justin's death, Jordie has been very much withdrawn, and extremely quiet.

Because of so much time spent at the hospital and with doctor visits at every turn, Craig and Shelia felt bad that they were not always there for Jordie, especially toward the end when Justin began to take a very bad turn. Craig was worried about him because *"he pretty much had to fend for himself and I could not be there. All Jordie kept saying was don't worry Dad, I'm fine."* Craig remarked that the biggest difference between Jordie and Justin, was that Justin always wore his heart on his sleeve, and was very emotional and talkative.

It was extremely hard on Jordie to serve as a pall bearer, knowing that he was carrying his brother. Craig said it was just out of the natural order of things, and that Jordie had great trouble with that. The last few months since Justin passed away, Jordie also has had an extremely difficult time walking near, or going into Justin's room at the house. Craig said that at first he had kept the door closed, because there were far too many memories inside to deal with. The door is now left open, but it is clear that the emotions within Jordie are not. Once again, Craig paused as he spoke of Justin's room, and began to emotionally well up in pain. After a few moments he said, *"as I walk near Justin's room, I keep having these feelings that he is still in the house. I almost expect him to jump around the corner and start joking like he always did. That is the hardest part of missing him so much."*

Craig talked about visitations to the cemetery and said he tries to go there every day. *"Talking to him there makes me feel his spirit, and if I am in a very down mood, he lifts me up a little, and makes me feel better. I know he is not suffering anymore, but it doesn't take away the burdens of the heart in missing someone you love so much."* When asked how Jordie has handled visits to the cemetery, Craig said that to the best of his knowledge, Jordie had not visited Justin's gravesite since the day of Justin's funeral. Craig believes that Jordie is just not ready yet, and respects the fact that he may need time to work out the pains, and emotions he is feeling.

As we spoke about Jordie, Craig softly said, *"I am worried about him all the time. He gets so quiet and I know he is hurting, and I feel helpless sometimes, but I keep my distance knowing this is going to take more time. He lost his brother and right now is not sure how to handle it. Over the last few months he has spent a lot of time with his grandparents, and Dr. Weil discussing some things, but his root pains hurt me too."* We spoke about healing and time, and of the emotions that teens may feel as they deal with a death in their family. I was one who related to that well as a young man, and shared those pains mourning the loss of both parents at a relatively young age. I believe Craig said it best when he sadly said, *"Jordie was lost without his brother."* He mentioned numerous times how much Jordie looked up to Justin as his big brother, and that he was grieving in ways that hurt him badly. The pains within his heart could be felt through the words of his father, who day by day, realizes the depths of this dreadful loss through the eyes of his youngest son. In time, Craig was hopeful that the heaviness of pain felt when Justin first died, will one day subside.

It was now late August of 2008 when I met Jordie and Craig at a nearby sandwich shop. I knew through Craig, that this was the first time that Jordie had been willing to open up and talk about Justin's death. We sat outside on a beautiful afternoon, and for the first few minutes we talked about just 'stuff' in general. Jordie had been working part time over the summer, and said he kept relatively busy. I asked Jordie what his plans

ON THE SEVENTH DAY OF APRIL....SUPERMAN DIED

were after his senior year passed at North Stafford High School. He said he was really looking forward to this last year as a Wolverine, and that after high school he was interested in a marketing, or business major in college. He also has interests in law enforcement.

Jordie was one year and three months younger than Justin. He was seventeen now, but he remembered younger days when he and Justin were in day care together. I laughed when Jordie described Justin at one point, as a seven year old *enforcer*! Jordie said, *"it was fine for Justin to mess with me, but if anyone else did it, Justin moved right in and put a stop to it."* He said that there was more than one time when other kids were harassing Jordie, and Justin would step around the corner and say, *"chill out and leave him alone or I will make you a part of the wall."* Mmmm...ah yes, the ever so subtle Justin Whitaker!

Jordie said that he and Justin always remained very close because of their ages. Jordie said that as kids, he and Justin would always rough house and wrestle, and do all the things that brothers do at home. He said, *"even when he was really sick, he was still always Justin. My dad had given Justin a bell in case something happened and he needed to get our attention. One day it was Justin being Justin. I was in the shower and heard the bell ringing away. I came flying around the corner and asked if he was o.k. He said he was fine. I shook my head and walked away, but a few minutes later I heard the bell ringing again. I came back and said, what's up with that? He had that big grin on his face and said, 'I'm just messing with you man, lighten up."* Jordie smiled telling that story, but I could tell that he was both nervous and sad talking about certain things.

As we started to discuss Justin after he was diagnosed with cancer, I could sense from Jordie's demeanor, that a different nerve had been struck, and that he knew we were about to discuss some uncomfortable subjects. Jordie said that, *"the hardest thing for me to see, was Justin lying motionless toward the end. But even during the earlier treatments, you could tell that it took so much out of his body. His emotions remained upbeat, but his body ached a lot of the time. Justin couldn't do too many things, so he became more dependent on me. I did a lot of his old chores and never minded. It was kind of like the roles were reversed."*

Craig, Jordie, and I talked about the first time when Justin was diagnosed with cancer. I asked Jordie what he remembered and he said, *"it was almost total disbelief. Once the treatments all started though, I knew that it was for real. Just seeing Justin lying there helpless and still sometimes, was very tough on me. He was always like a 'Jack-In-The-Box' toy, zipping around the house and fooling around non-stop, that I could not believe he was now basically motionless. To me it felt like his freedom had been completely taken away."*

In November of 2007, when Justin underwent his bone marrow transplant procedure, Jordie knew through his father that it was a last ditch effort. Dr. Weil had explained to the family that the bone marrow transplant was necessary if Justin's life was to be saved. Doctors all agreed that it was a 50/50 chance that Justin would even be strong enough to survive the transplant. I asked Jordie how he felt upon hearing that Justin may die if the procedure was not successful, Jordie began tearing up, trying to hold it all in. He took some time to gather himself and said, *"I guess we knew that Justin could die, but it just seemed all too unreal for me. I had in my head that some kind of miracle would arise and save him. I think Justin believed that too."* Craig commented with high praise once again for Dr. Weil and her staff at the Inova Fairfax ICU. Craig added, *"Dr. Weil said that Justin was so special to her and the entire unit. At one point, Dr. Weil told us that Justin touched her in ways that patients normally do not. She was Justin's primary doctor, and could not be there all the time, but for the most part, she was. She became a part of our family. I think the doctors and nurses took Justin in because he not only survived the transplant, but dug in for another five months before his body just got too tired of fighting."*

As we finished talking about Justin's bone marrow transplant, Jordie perked up and said, *"one thing that amazed me was that one of Justin's nurses, Kelly, had been trying to have a baby. She used to sit and talk to Justin all the time, and Justin would tell Kelly, "don't worry Kelly, you will have kids." That to me was pretty amazing, because in a way, Justin and Kelly had this tight bond at the hospital, and you just felt that his words were the truth about her having a baby one day soon."* I asked Jordie if he had ever talked with Justin about the bone marrow transplant, and if he was scared? Jordie said, *"there was something inside of me that said he would make it through the procedure. I had no doubt about that. But, then there was the other side of me that told me in a way, to prepare myself for the worst. I talked with Justin at home before the transplant."* There was a long pause and I glanced at Jordie with tears running down his face as he said,

ON THE SEVENTH DAY OF APRIL....SUPERMAN DIED

"Justin asked me what I thought about the procedure. I told him that it is not what we want to see happen, but we will get through it like we always do. Then Justin said, "if I have a kid someday, I am going to name him Jordie you know." I had all I could do to keep it in at the table, as Jordie and Craig both shed tears together, as soon as those sad words came out of Jordie's mouth. You could almost hear Justin saying that to Jordie right then and there. In one other conversation, Justin told Jordie, *"I don't want you to ruin your life over me Jordie. Don't you miss out on anything worrying about me."*

Jordie reflected on time in the hospital before Justin suffered the seizure and went into the coma. Jordie sadly said, *"Justin and I never really had the chance for a one on one talk before he died. There were times though, when he would see me crying, and would say in that same Justin tone, "Jordie, why are you crying? I beat this damn thing before. I will beat it again." The best thing for me was, even if he was in a lot of pain, Justin would do something funny in his room that reminded me of times when we played together as kids. He would slap me around, or make me laugh flirting with the nurses. He would always do something funny that brought the old Justin back."*

I asked Jordie what he recalled when he was told that Justin had little time left to live. Jordie said, *"my dad and I drove up to the hospital after he talked to Dr. Weil. She explained that Justin would eventually be removed from life support."* At this point, again with tears in his eyes, Craig interjected by saying, *"I don't know what's harder, losing a child in an accident, or having something prolonged. You still lose someone you love, and it breaks your heart into a million pieces."* Once again tears flowed at our table from all of us. Jordie paused and said, *"I just never got the chance to tell him how much I loved and cared about him as my brother. As I watched him take his last breath, it didn't seem real. When I was alone in a quiet spot after, I thought of this handshake we used to do as kids. It was always something a little different, and Justin would change the rhythm of it, but it was ours. Justin used to sing these silly songs when we did the handshake, and it occurred to me after that we would never share that again. I know that one day though, we will share that handshake. I know it."* The three of us talked about those last couple days in ICU, and wondered about whether Justin could hear all the visitors talking to him privately. Jordie said, *"I think Justin did hear us talking to him. Why be negative and say that he couldn't hear us? He heard us."*

Our last few minutes drifted to talks about a quiet house now with Justin gone, and of the gravesite. Craig told me that Justin's room, with the exception of boxes of some of his clothes, remained untouched to this day. Craig repeated what he had said earlier, in that for the first month after Justin died, the door to his bedroom was kept closed. Craig said, *"sometimes the hardest thing was in the morning. I would say good morning to Jordie, and then almost out of habit, I wanted to push Justin's door open and wish him the same thing. That was so hard knowing he was gone."* Jordie said that he never went in Justin's room right away, but now he will go in and sit on the bed, and remember all the fun we had in there. Jordie said, *"it seems so quiet now, but I have flashbacks of us wrestling, and pulling pranks on each other. I close my eyes and see Justin running around the corner after me, and I smile at all the good memories. That is what I choose to remember now, not the sad times at the end."*

In somewhat of a surprise to Craig I suppose, Jordie revealed at the table that he had indeed, visited Justin's gravesite. He said, *"the morning after his funeral, I went there with some friends. There is some humor too in a way. It was about 2 a.m., and it was really strange. It had just started to drizzle out lightly, and I said hey, what's up with that Justin? The drizzle stopped. Then it started to rain a little harder, and a couple claps of thunder hit, and I said hey Justin, do you want us to leave? Then it finally rained hard and steady. We jumped in the cars, and as I looked back toward Justin's grave, we all laughed about how Justin had a hand in the sudden bad weather...just another prank as always."*

As we were ending our talk, I looked at Jordie and asked him how he sees his future, and where this all leaves him. Jordie very maturely said, *"Justin used to always tell me, you will graduate high school and everything will be fine. He would always say, "if you don't make it Jordie, I won't make it." I'll make it in life now because of him. At the viewing, as I looked at Justin in the casket, it was not the Justin I knew but the person inside was. I remembered thinking as I looked down at him, about the long fight he had with his cancer. Now when there are rough days for me, I think about how he handled things during the worst of times. That way I am able to keep it all together. Every day now seems to get a little easier because I keep things in better perspective."*

There were a couple of things that very few people know about, as it related to Justin's viewing. Craig and I talked about the massive crowds that kept pouring into the funeral home to say goodbye to Justin for the very last time. There were some who never knew him, yet it was clearly a gesture of human kindness to make an appearance for a young man who touched so many. The Whitaker family remarked to me that Justin's viewing mirrored an event worthy of a dignitary, police officer, firefighter, or one from the military lost in the line of duty.

Lost within all of it were two acts of love that virtually went unnoticed. Seeking a private moment alone with Justin, Courtney was able to kneel down, and surreptitiously remove her class ring, and slip it inside Justin's casket. The Whitaker and Crews families were astounded by her love, yet not surprised at how she expressed her own goodbye to someone she loved so very much. Courtney kept Justin's class ring as a bond forever…each having a piece of their school experience, and more importantly, of each other.

Barbara Whitaker, Justin's grandmother, also knelt and had private words as she stared down at Justin's peaceful expression, knowing he was finally free of all his pain. Barbara too, offered Justin a special gift. She slowly took out a beautiful silver bracelet that Justin had given her after a visit to the Baseball Hall of Fame in Cooperstown. She whispered her prayers of love, and slid the bracelet into the pocket of his suit. Barbara sought to return a gift, to the young man she loved who offered her a lifetime of gifts.

In this fall of 2008, Justin's sister Amber Janney, now had five months to deal with the traumas associated with Justin's death. It was clear from the moment we began talking though, that many wounds had yet to heal. Amber and I talked of Justin's youth, as she mentored her brothers, and often times, served as the chief babysitter. She said, *"I remember when Justin was about five and Jordie was four. When I took them to stores, they would dart away and hide underneath clothes racks. They drove me crazy. I was eight years older, and have great memories of the three of us at the playground. To be perfectly honest, I was not truly happy unless I had them running all around me. We had fun during those early days."* Amber's pains in missing her brother throughout our conversation, lent itself to heartfelt tears as she remembered all of the good times, while dredging up the darkened moments as well. Even when Justin was a young boy of two, Amber spoke of how Justin was always a very special boy. She said, *"even at two years old, Justin was just so* loveable, and caring. Similar to how he later treated others when he was so sick, even as a young boy, he would always worry about everyone and wanted to know if they were o.k. To me as I watched him play with Jordie and other kids, he seemed so much more mature and ahead of his time. As he started to get older, you could see that baseball was a primary love of his. He always drove himself so hard. He learned the game and seemed to pay attention to details that most kids wouldn't. He had this intensity that a lot of people may not have understood, especially when he got so frustrated, but that was just Justin being Justin."

As time moved on, Amber lamented that time spent with Justin was often limited. He was a growing teenager, was always on the run, and had also started seeing Courtney. Amber related that, *"when Justin was in his freshman, and sophomore years, we would sit and talk, and be open about basically everything. We would talk about his friends and what he was doing, and everything was pretty much fair game. When he had his knee injury, it appeared minor, and just a small setback for Justin. Then doctors stunned us and diagnosed him with cancer. I look back now and remember how I knew something was wrong when Justin first complained of chest pains. He never complained about anything…ever. If Justin told you he was in pain, then you can believe he was. He was having a really hard time breathing, and at Potomac Hospital, they ordered a chest x-ray. That is when the cancer was discovered, and because it was tied to his breathing, he was rushed from there to Inova Fairfax Hospital for surgery. I guess you could say that I moved into an immediate state of shock, because his trouble breathing turned into the doctors finding a large mass in his lymph nodes. From that point on, my mom and I, along with Courtney, spent the majority of the time by Justin's side. Even at the very beginning when Justin was told he had cancer, he would always say, "sis, don't you worry. I will handle all of this." He would be lying there so still, but his smile never left him. He told everyone who talked to him that there was no way cancer was beating him!"*

There was incredible sadness in Justin's July 2006 diagnosis of cancer, yet it arose within Amber's life on a whole different front. When Justin and his family were told that he had cancer, it was only twenty days before Amber was to be married to her soon to be husband, Steven. Justin and Jordie were excited that they would be walking Amber down the aisle. Justin was in the hospital for two weeks, and he constantly told the doctors and nurses that, *"I have to get out of here. I have to walk my sister down*

Superman—Justin Whitaker.

Justin...ever the dashing gentleman.

Jordie, Dad, & Justin—A loving trifecta.

Amber's Wedding: *Rear Left to Right—Shelia, Justin, Delores, Jordie, Amber, Steven, and Front—Charles.*

Barbara, Justin, and Darrell celebrate graduation.

Courtney and Justin at Virginia Beach.

Zac and Justin…the truest meaning of best friends.

Dance
Love
Sing
Live
LIFE
JUSTIN LEE WHITAKER
SEPT. 7, 1989 - APRIL 7, 2008
LOVING SON, BROTHER, GRANDSON
AND SPECIAL FRIEND

Justin "Forever Home" at North Stafford High School.

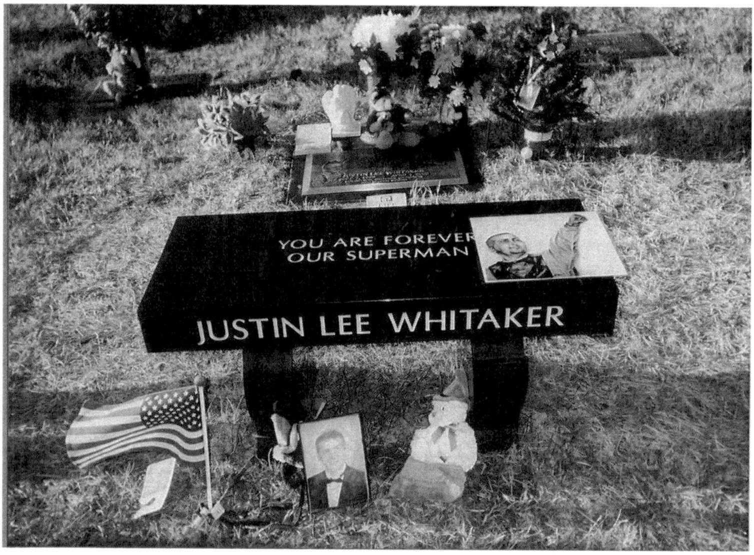
YOU ARE FOREVER
OUR SUPERMAN
JUSTIN LEE WHITAKER

Justin in a proud pose at the 2002 Cooperstown Dreams Park Tournament.

VIRGINIA THUNDER
#2002642　　July 13, 2002　　Virginia

2002: Team Photo-Cooperstown, N.Y.

LEFT to RIGHT: Zac, Craig, Cal Ripken Jr., and Jordie talking baseball about the legend that was Justin Whitaker

Courtney and Justin in happier days.

JUSTIN and COURTNEY'S FOOTPRINTS (FLIP FLOPS), IN THE SAND.......

Footprints in the sand at Virginia Beach… "Promises Made."

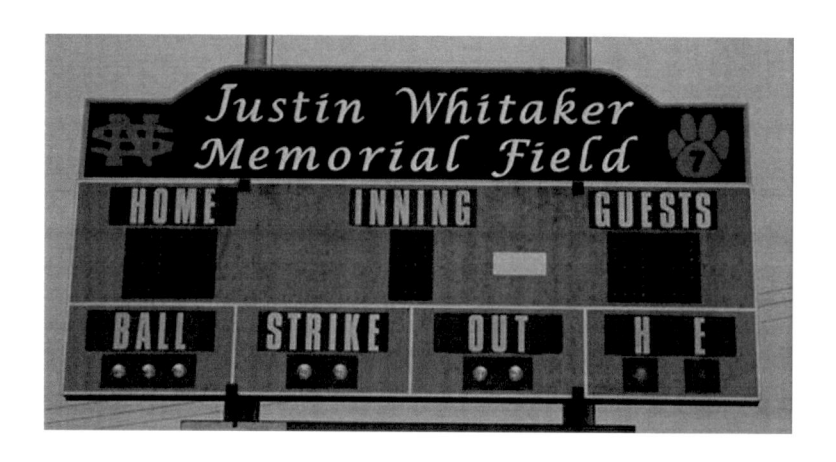

NSHS baseball field renamed after Justin.

the aisle to get married." Justin was given a day pass from Inova, and he did walk me down that aisle. The one beautiful memory I have of Justin and the wedding, was how he danced with everyone. He had just gone through the first horrible round of chemo treatments, and had his bone marrow biopsy done too. But right now, I can close my eyes and see him dancing and smiling. He was worn out and drained by the end of the night, but he made our day extra special."

Amber related to me that Justin, and everyone around him had high hopes after his initial diagnosis. The care and treatments lasted for nine months, and Justin then moved into a remission stage for another nine months. Amber said that hope was suddenly dashed when the cancer again returned with a vengeance. Amber said that *"it now seemed like everything happened in chain reaction. The cancer had spread throughout his chest and neck, and within a short time, doctors said that a bone marrow transplant was necessary. It was November of 2007, and the procedure was done at Children's Hospital in D.C. My mom and I spent almost the entire time with him for about two weeks. He went through hard core radiation and lost all of his hair. I think at that point, it was the weakest I had ever seen Justin look. His cheeks were very puffy, but I used to try to keep his spirits up, telling him he looked like a little chipmunk. To watch him receive the radiation treatments was brutal. He was weak to begin with, and had to stand up the entire time. Both of his arms were extended straight out on either side, and I commented to my mother that Justin looked like he was ready for a crucifix. Spiritually, I had this Justin and Jesus tie as I saw that. These treatments put so much stress on him, and were at least forty five minutes each time. The radiation was so intense that he had unbearable mouth sores. He couldn't eat many foods, and he seemed to be always sick. I remember him telling me about three months before he died that, "I have the fight sis, but my body can't take this much longer."*

As Amber recalled all of Justin's treatments, her eyes welled with tears as she seemingly felt his pains again as he battled through torturous radiation. Her talks with Justin at that juncture, became far more personal. She said, *"Justin always had his buddies around, and his dad to talk about sports and all that stuff. I chose the opportunity to speak from the heart and talk about everything else he felt, including his cancer, so that he could vent and not feel alone. Courtney was amazing the entire time too. She never left Justin's side and felt closer to him when there at the hospital too. But after Justin went through all of* his radiation, and then the bone marrow transplant ended up failing, the chore was to always try to find food that Justin could handle three times a day. His throat and mouth were so sore, that we always kept him supplied with milkshakes and slurpees, which he loved. Trust me though, there were times he would crave ice cream, and his favorite...cookies. I don't know how he did it, but he always managed to eat those cookies. I think the bone marrow failure really hit him hard. The bone marrow was first producing stem cells, and suddenly it stopped, and he needed transfusions, which really took a lot out of him. Justin was very scared then, and became really mad that this sickness was beating him. He was dying to be home for Christmas, and then get back to school. As I look back now, it seemed like Justin was always in the hospital for most, if not all of our family birthdays too. But, even as sick as he was, if someone's birthday was coming up, he never forgot to make it special, and have a gift waiting no matter what. He was in so much pain, but he loved everyone so much, that he always felt he had to do something special for someone. Here he was in absolute agony at times, and his mind drifted off wondering what gift he needed to buy...amazing."

As the new year of 2008 rolled in, the Whitaker family, and all those who loved Justin, received news they never wanted to hear. Amber remembers the doctors messages like it was yesterday. She sadly said, "they told all of us to do everything we ever wanted to do with him, and to not put anything off. The reality of it all hit us when the doctors told us that Justin could be gone at any moment from an infection tied to his bone marrow failure. It was so shocking, and almost seemed unreal. We kept saying, this cannot be happening. I remember one day when Justin and I were alone after being told this news and he said, "do you think I will know if something bad is happening when it comes?" All I could tell him was that he had great doctors and that they would be able to explain everything. My heart was breaking. I guess I always thought that there would be more time. The hardest thing for me is that much later, by the time everything shut down in his body, I never had the chance to tell him goodbye. I needed more private conversations with him. I also knew though, that if he did have a short time to live, that I would do all I could to keep his spirits up." Amber paused and tears welled up in her eyes as she slowly said, "after Justin had seizures and his temperature spiked at Mary Washington Hospital in Fredericksburg, my mom and I were with Justin in his room. The nurses were trying to get his fever down, and my mom and I both tried to softly touch his face, and Justin groaned and said, "don't

ON THE SEVENTH DAY OF APRIL...SUPERMAN DIED

touch my head...it hurts so bad." The doctors later told us that Justin had developed an infection within his brain, and they started to administer pain meds. I looked at Justin and he was in so much agony. I said you're not going anywhere. You have a lot of fight left. Justin lay still with his eyes closed, and after a while I told him I was leaving, because they were readying to transport him to Inova Fairfax. I said take it easy Justin. I love you. Justin squeezed my had and softly said, "I love you too." That was the last time my brother said anything to anyone." Ambers tears told me that she had just brought back those last moments.

To lighten things a little, I asked if there was something special, or heart warming about Justin's times in the hospital. She said, "I think it had to be just before he was going to give Courtney her promise ring. I was there when he was about to order it. He was so excited and suddenly he started quizzing me. He said, "sis, how do you think I can ask her," or "how can I surprise her?" All I said to Justin was to speak from the heart, and tell me what you think you will say? He looked at me and said, "I want to promise Courtney that one day I will marry her." In my mind I always keep hearing him say that. I always wonder if he knew he was getting sicker by the day, and that his "wanting" to marry Courtney, was said because he knew somehow that he would never realistically have that chance because of his cancer. Just hearing him say that in my mind is so painful sometimes. I also have great, fun memories of him whenever he was discharged from the hospital after stays there, or right after treatments. I would pick him up, and he would get in my car and we would crank the music up loud and sing. We would laugh and really get into it. Cars would pull up beside us and think we were nuts, but you know what? We could care less. Whenever I am down, I think about him smiling and laughing in my car, and I feel closer to him"

Amber let me see a side of Justin that I had not felt from others as she described having a conversation with him about the hospital DNR ('Do Not Resuscitate') order. Amber said, "we talked about all of this, and about what would happen if he went into a coma long before it happened. One day I asked him, do you ever want to come back as someone other than who you really are if they bring you back to life? I mentioned that he could have brain damage, and some of the effects of that. Justin looked at me and said, "I don't care what happens to me after, but if the doctors and nurses have the chance to save me, then that is what I want done." Justin had a belief that unless every effort was not expended to save his life, God may not save him either, and he would go to hell. I told him, Justin, that *will never happen, just because of all the lives you have touched. He looked at me with the saddest eyes and said, "look at all the little kids here. If I am to be taken that is fine, but it is wrong to see these kids taken."*

My time spent with Amber was winding down, and I actually felt guilty bringing so many painful things up again, and asking her to recall days best forgotten. Yet, she seemed to be the type of person that felt more at ease reveling in memories as the big sister at playgrounds, playing hide-and-seek in stores, and yes, in dreadful hospital settings too. Reflecting on deeply personal thoughts, Amber said, *"one day I told Justin, you know that you don't have to be so tough and strong, a 'Superman' for everyone if you don't want to. He knew that, but inside he* **had to be** *that Superman because fighting forward was all he knew. One day when he was in his bed and in terrible pain, I watched as a tear rolled down his cheek, and all he said was, "don't worry about me sis. I'm going to be fine." That is who my brother was, deflecting his own pain and taking all of yours in. There was so many special things about him, and right now…today, I am sure that I only knew half of the wonderful things there was about who he really was, and what he meant to everyone. There were nights when he called and woke me, telling me he was in so much pain, and he asked me to pray with him. We prayed together, and he was able to drift off to sleep. I know that as soon as he died, he was in a far better place. I think all the time about those last words spoken at Mary Washington Hospital, before he later fell into a coma. I remember turning toward him as I was leaving and said, see you later Justin. I know that someday I will, without a doubt."*

Justin's aunt, Gail Woodham, in a touching open letter to Justin, spoke of his dreadful illness, while poignantly focusing on the brilliance of his eternal rest. Gail wrote…

Dear Justin,

"When I heard you were sick, I prayed for God to heal you. I prayed that God would give your Mom, Jordan, and Amber strength to accept this terrible disease that hurt your body. As my voice quivered amidst sobs, I told your Mom to tell you never to give up. When I last saw you over the summer, you looked like an ordinary guy. You never once complained as a dreadful disease coursed through your body. Your eyes were like brilliant stars, and your smile was worth a million dollars. And when you were close to leaving us, I asked you to promise me you would never give up. You

simply said, "o.k. Aunt Gail, I promise." I know now that God had your life mapped out and planned. I know here on earth, losing someone is never easy to accept, but we garner strength because of the words taught to us by God. "His Will Be Done." Your life light will shine forever bright within our hearts. Until we meet again, rest in peace my beloved Justin. For God truly had an angel walking with us on earth. Thank you for letting us love you, and for brightening all of our lives." Aunt Gail

Shelia Whitaker's parents, Delores and Charles Harmon, sought to have their thoughts about Justin to be short and sweet, yet touching to the soul. They always remembered Justin as a child talking about the bible, asking lots of questions, and singing in church. When they found out he was sick, they had to put their faith in God. Aunt Dee Dee used to love singing songs to him to boost his spirits. Dee Dee said, *"I would read 'God's Promises' to him from the Bible. I knew Justin would continue to fight until God was ready to take him home."* Collectively, the Harmon's and Aunt Dee Dee felt that God's light would shine through Justin, and lead him to wherever he was to be taken. Dee Dee said it best by saying, *"Justin has reached more lives in his eighteen years than* most people could ever imagine to do in a lifetime."

The Harmon's offered Justin this solemn goodbye;

Dear Justin,
"*We all miss you, but we know you have a new body now. You are with God, Jesus, and the Holy Angels. You were just so tired here on this earth. We will see you soon."*
I have fought a good fight. I have finished my course. I have kept the faith. Henceforth, there is laid up for me a crown of righteousness, with the Lord as the righteous judge. Shall give me at that day, and not to me only. But unto all of them that love his appearing. (2nd Timothy: 4, 7, and 8)
Love, Grandpa and Grandma Harmon

On a very chilly morning in the last week of February of 2009, I met with Justin's grandparents, Barbara and Darrell Whitaker. It was immediately evident that this meeting, with Craig in attendance as well, would be extremely emotional for everyone. Everyone surrounding Justin from the point when his cancer was diagnosed, to the last moments of his passing, knew that Barbara and Darrell marched with him every step of the way. To say they served as primary caretakers, and were equally responsible for his care and welfare, would be treading on that subject lightly.

Barbara and Darrell reflected back on the happiest of times, seeing Justin and Jordie joined at the hip, doing all the fun things that boys are meant to do. One time Darrell remembered rounding the corner into Justin's room. He watched as Justin used the mattress of his crib like a trampoline and was close to clearing the rails. Darrell said, *"I guess you could always say that he had a hyper side to him, but as far as energy went, I think he stole the patent on it."* Darrell said that even as a young boy, Justin's love of baseball was clear to anyone who watched him. Darrell recalled a young man who not only held a love for the game, but respected its history. Darrell remarked, *"some people mindlessly played the game, but never Justin. He played hard always, and his intensity and desire to become better and better was evident anytime you saw him with a bat in his hand, or a glove as he played catch. His admiration for the game of baseball was incredible."* Darrell added, *"I close my eyes now and see this skinny eight year old, running in the yard, or playing catch and it seems like yesterday. But there was another side of Justin that was amazing. He was an admirer of Civil War times, and he dug into the history of all the wars with a penchant that was very unusual for a boy his age. There was a real funny story one time. There was a Civil War re-enactment with an old gentleman imitating General Robert E. Lee. Here is Justin locked in on every word as he described his actions at the Battle of Gettysburg. All of a sudden Justin perked up and asked, "General Lee, why would you ever decide to attack down the middle like you did, rather than try some type of flank attack?" My God I laughed inside and trust me, the General was very flabbergasted. Justin knew his history and all the battles and had the good General on that one."*

Barbara patiently waited as Darrell's tales of Justin's youthful times waned down, and you could sense an aura of sadness surrounding all of us. Barbara spoke the entire time in an even manner, yet you noticed tears welling in her eyes as she remembered both the best of, and the worst of times. Barbara said, *"Justin was simply a very loving, caring, compassionate, polite boy from minute one. He was just so kind, always offering his hugs and kisses at times when you needed them the most. But like Darrell said, there were always two sides of him. His intensity playing baseball was immense, but then he would switch gears later and you would see this loving soul of a boy who always wanted to see you happy. That attribute never, ever left him up until the time of his death. There was one occasion when Justin cut his head and needed stitches. But he had so much energy and was so strong, that nobody could hold him down to have him taken care of. His physical strength and intensity, was a complete 360 degrees from his loving heart and kindness. That is what I miss the most…his love."*

Barbara and Darrell remembered so many fun trips from days gone by, watching Justin compete in AAU baseball tournaments. They both spoke of *"literally seeing him grow into this chiseled athlete before our eyes. He was the same at home. We always watched him wrestle with Jordie and at times tease and torment, but he was incredibly protective of him too.* **Nobody** *messed with Jordie in Justin's presence…nobody!"* As we softly talked, it was quite clear that Barb and Darrell Whitaker were self-described *"parent figures"* from the start. Darrell proudly remarked that, *"Barbara and I agree that being around Justin and Jordie so much was a gift for us. We were like parents in many ways, and always seemed to be around the boys as they grew up right in front of us."*

As we wound through the adolescent years, it was inevitable that I felt the need to move fast forward to a time that Barbara and Darrell would rather forget about. I can honestly say that from glancing at Craig, and seeing tears welled up in the eyes of two loving grandparents, that I too would soon possess that lump in the throat feeling. Barbara Whitaker, through all of the trials and tribulations associated with Justin's cancer, was no stranger to tragedies within the medical field. Barbara recently retired after thirty years of medical experience, with significant time as a Physician's Assistant. The George Washington graduate later opened her own practice before deciding that retirement was looming. I felt this immense sadness from within as Barbara began to talk about Justin's diagnosis of cancer when he was sixteen.

Barbara said, *"Justin had a knee injury he was dealing with, and shortly after that as he was recovering, he complained about a lump in the front of his throat. Darrell and I always took the kids to appointments because Craig worked, and we always enjoyed doing that and making sure they were squared away. I took Justin to his physical therapy appointment for his knee, and within a short period of time he had difficulty breathing. I remember seeing him struggling with weight as he attempted a bench press. It was at that moment when I saw the mass protruding from the front of his throat area. Early that evening, Justin had trouble swallowing his food, so Craig took him to Potomac Hospital in Woodbridge, Virginia. The staff gave him a CT scan. His mom Shelia was there as well, and overheard one of the doctors talking about seeing a "huge mass." I think Craig had passed on to the doctor what my role had been in the medical field, and asked the doctor to call me and explain what was found."* As Barbara fought to continue talking, it was as if she was hearing that dreadful phone call over again. I glanced at Darrell who had to glance away from me because he was emotionally struggling, and waited as Barbara's heartfelt aches subsided. Wiping tears from her eyes, Barbara softly spoke. She said, *"I will never in my life forgot the doctor's words. He said Mrs. Whitaker, I'm so sorry to tell you this, but Justin has a huge mass in his chest."* With her past professional experiences, Barbara related to me that she thought that Justin's symptoms first mirrored Mononucleosis. Barbara remembered that date of June 11, 2006 clearly as well. The tests went on to reveal large masses in Justin's chest and throat.

Justin was immediately rushed to Potomac Hospital, and then to the Inova Fairfax Hospital in Fairfax, Virginia. At this point, Craig looked at me and said, *"on the way to Fairfax, I explained in the ambulance to Justin that he had to be taken there for more tests so specialists could determine what was going on. Justin turned with the saddest eyes and said, "Dad, I'm sorry for ever talking bad to you...ever. I'm sorry for ever making you angry for anything I had done wrong." There were tears streaming down his face and I ached for him. Here he was being told that he was very sick and was so scared, yet he was strong enough to apologize to me for something he felt he did to hurt me."*

Barbara went on to say that from that point on, she and Darrell basically took Justin to all his appointments. Barb said, *"we were retired and Darrell and I never treated this situation as any kind of burden. We would have done nothing differently."* Barbara went on to talk about the 1:30 a.m. phone call she received from Craig that literally, *"changed our world forever."* Barbara plainly said, *"our whole world shattered after that phone call. I rarely*

ON THE SEVENTH DAY OF APRIL....SUPERMAN DIED

ever break down but I did after that phone call." The calendar flipped pages backward into August of 2006 for the Whitakers. Justin was aggressively treated with chemotherapy, and there was hope that because of his age and strength, he would win this fight. Again, Barbara with incredible recollection remarked, *"I will never forget dates, and it was August 26th when I drove Justin home from an appointment. Justin was getting out of the car and looked at me with the saddest eyes and said, "look Grandma," as he touched the front of his throat. He had a golf ball-sized mass protruding again, and without hesitation he was rushed to Inova Fairfax Hospital again. He had radiation treatments that were brutal, because at this point, doctors needed to shrink the mass before they could go forward with a bone marrow procedure. Dr. Weil from Inova did a nationwide search for a compatible bone marrow donor, and found only two that were a 100% match to Justin. Dr. Weil informed the family that Dr. Terry Frye from Children's Hospital would be performing the bone marrow transplant."*

Once again, it was quite evident that Barbara had to pause as she described the private hell Justin was going through. Fighting back tears Barbara said, *"it was now mid-November of 2006, and before the bone marrow procedure could be done, Justin's body would be punished by exhaustive waves of direct radiation treatments on not only the mass, but throughout his entire body. There were also two very painful chemo treatments as well that left Justin wracked in pain. It crushed us to see him lose all of his body hair, including his eyelashes. Justin was a trooper the entire time. That boy never complained, but you could see so much pain in his eyes."*

The calendar sorrowfully moved into a new year of 2008. On January 2nd, Justin was scheduled for a Proton Emission Tomography (PET) test. This was a critical point in Justin's care, and Barbara knew that this would be the tell all as to how Justin's body reacted to the bone marrow transplant, following all of the chemo, and radiation treatments. Barbara said, *"the PET exam basically shows doctors if there are any masses remaining within the body. I remember the doctor telling us news that absolutely killed all of us. He said that they found three spots of cancer under both of Justin's arms, and behind the vena cava. To me, I knew deep inside my heart that this finding meant Justin's life was almost over. I think following this time, I lost five or six pounds almost immediately. I felt absolutely helpless."* Barbara's tears returned and she could not speak anymore, and we were all briefly overcome by intense pains of the heart. Darrell, who could barely control his emotions now, recalled that day with intense clarity. He said, *"the doctor told all of us that there was three paths that could be taken. He said, we can keep Justin here under hospital care so that he is comfortable and highly medicated. He also said that he could be kept in the hospital free of medicines and basically left alone, or he could go home and simply enjoy his life, while continuing treatments."*

I must say that at this point, all four of us at this busy coffee shop were overcome with grief as Darrell discontinued his story so that he could wipe his eyes. People walking by and around us sensed something bad was being discussed, yet held no idea how much pain had re-surfaced at this lonely table. I felt this need to rush outside and suck in some cold winter air, but we all remained intact as Darrell regained his composure. I had to glance away from Darrell now because I felt this incredible internal heat arising in my body…painful to the core. Darrell said, *"I was all alone with Justin at one point, and he turned to me with tears in his eyes and said "Grandpa, it really hurts when doctors tell you that you are going to die."* As soon as Darrell echoed those words of Justin's, the tears flowed again and the unbearable pain that seemingly enveloped all of us returned with vicious fury. Suddenly, I saw Justin as a dutiful AAU baseball player again, but not one with an illness. I needed that image to continue doing this interview. I conjured up any thoughts that were necessary in order to rid my mind of this crushing sadness. At this point, Craig had to relieve Darrell from his painful recitation. Craig added, *"that night when we got Justin home, he turned to me and said, "what do I do now Dad?" I told him that he had to live life to the fullest now. I will never forget what Justin said next. He said, "then damn it Dad, that is what I am going to do."* Justin Whitaker was given two months at the most to live the life he fought to save. It was more than evident to everyone that Justin would not enjoy a June graduation with his classmates, and plans were hurriedly made by the family and North Stafford High School brethren to expedite everything.

Barbara and Darrell were amazed as to the 'man' they saw in Justin Whitaker from that moment on. His loving, compassionate nature remained well intact as they watched him stroll over to nursing stations after appointments greeting all. There were *always* the 'Justin Whitaker hugs' involved, as nurses took him to a room that they referred to as

"Justin's Room" whenever he was in for treatments. Darrell related to me another poignant memory shared with Dr. Weil from Inova's ICU. Marcie had asked Justin what he wanted to do with what was left of his life. Darrell said Dr. Weil related that he answered saying, *"by far, giving Courtney her 'Promise Ring' was something he **had** to do. Then I want to stand tall and graduate high school."* Darrell broke down and wept as those sullen memories washed over his mind.

As we sipped coffee, we all needed a break to breathe a bit. Without question, this day was one of the hardest personally for me. This was *not* your ordinary set of grandparents here. This was a couple unlike most I had met in the stage of life they were in. There is no doubt that all grandparents would do all that was possible to help a grandchild, and ease the pain of their own children. But this was different. Barbara and Darrell Whitaker went above and beyond their dutiful roles, and the truest images of caretakers to me, moved far beyond even those seen in modern health care today. Justin Whitaker was admired, and loved by health care professionals, and anyone around them, because you could not help but to feel this aura of love emanating from family, and those closest to Justin. Barbara and Darrell Whitaker added the upmost clarity to both life and loss, and in this brief span of time of pain and remembrance, I too was captured by their spiritual love and affection. In my mind, Justin *had* returned to me, especially now. He was wearing his Virginia Thunder uniform, and later he was adorned in the colors of North Stafford High School with glove in hand, patrolling the outfield. Barbara and Darrell brought that all back for me and saved me from a sense of utter agony at this moment in time.

Darrell recalled something else during Justin's fight that held poignancy beyond words. He said that back in September of 2007, Justin revealed to him what hurt the most. It was at that point when Justin found out that because of his massive radiation and chemo treatments, he could never father a child. Doctors informed him following a test that Justin sought himself, that because of the intense treatments, all of his sperm had been killed in the process. Darrell remarked, *"here is a young man who on his own volition, asked for a test to see if he could ever be a father. He wanted that test because his plan was to hopefully freeze his sperm and save it. Justin felt that there may be a time in the future if Courtney never married, that the sperm could be utilized to give Court* **his baby!** *When the call came in from the doctor about the test results, I gave Barb the phone because Justin couldn't bear the news if bad. After Barbara talked to the doctor, who confirmed that Justin's sperm was not viable, she hung up and told Justin. He was so angry that he reared back with his hand and smacked the back side of it against the hospital bedrail."* The weight of this moment was palpable as Barbara added, *"I have never seen Justin this angry. He was absolutely, positively crushed by this news. He went into what I would call a rage of immense sadness."* Craig recalled that day well as well saying that Justin said while crying, *"I'm never, ever going to be able to have babies Dad. I'm never going to ever be a* **real** *Dad. I let Courtney down."* All I could say to Justin as he cried and was so angry was that he fought every single day to live since his cancer was found, and he **was** the best man I had ever known."

Barbara and Darrell chose now to reflect on a time in October of 2006, when the truest meaning of selflessness became evident as it related to Justin's dreadful illness. The Outback restaurant off of Rt. 610 in N. Stafford, Virginia hosted a fundraiser that brought deep emotion into the hearts of the entire Whitaker family, and all who generously supported them. The Outback Manager, LaDonna Lenzini, graciously welcomed Justin and an entire community into the restaurant for what Darrell called, *"an amazing act of kindness."* There were two hundred tickets originally printed for the event, yet there was one slight problem. Over four hundred people showed their loving support for Justin on this night. Darrell remarked that, *"for some people it took over forty five minutes to even get into the restaurant, but there was this feeling from everyone that time was never an issue. Nobody was burdened at all. What was really something though, was when LaDonna and her incredible staff informed us that the Outback had chosen to donate all of the food for Justin's night. What really stunned us next was that all of the waitresses, waiters, and bartenders also refused to accept any tips from anyone. In this day and age, we were all taken aback by the affection and kindness shown to Justin and everyone who loved him. I believe we were able to raise about $6500.00 that night, but the heartfelt emotions coming out of it were even more amazing."*

There was another unexpected gesture that night at the Outback, that again, made Darrell and Barbara tear up. A Lieutenant Colonel from the Marines had finally made his way to the front near Justin, and when it was his turn to greet him, he shook his hand and gave him a check for $150.00. Darrell trembled slightly and softly said, *"here is a complete stranger who makes out a check for Justin, and was proud to have waited his turn to meet him. He told Justin that he was a cancer survivor, and that he had recently returned home after hiking across the country. The Colonel then added that next year he intended to hike across Canada. You could see that look in Justin's eyes. It was an expression of hope, and fight to go the distance. You know, to this day, I never found out the name of that Colonel. All I know is that he was just another example of the type of people who cared about Justin, and who were deeply respectful of his courageous fight."*

Barbara Whitaker talked sullenly and painfully moved the calendar up to March 23, 2008. Once again, the Outback restaurant served as the place of choice to celebrate Courtney's eighteenth birthday party. Barbara said, *"it seemed like everything was flying fast now. Justin was growing more tired by the day, and his inability to eat and swallow food was painful to watch. That night Justin ordered three lobster tails, but barely ate one half of only one. His appetite was waning badly, yet on Courtney's special night, we watched him as he laughed all night, and somehow held that special grin on his face for everyone. After that night he had doctor's appointments in readiness for his planned 'Promise Ring' trip to Virginia Beach. On Sunday night at about 8:00 or 9:00 p.m., Justin called Darrell and I just to say they had a good time and were on the way home. What I noticed in his voice though, was very disturbing. He sounded absolutely exhausted and was slurring badly. That night when he got home, Craig told us how scared he was and we were both so worried. His ankles and face had also become very swollen. With my job, I had the feeling right away that he was showing signs of complete liver failure."*

Craig could clearly feel that night return as he said, *"Justin was so scared that he wanted me to lay down beside him. He said, "Dad, I am so afraid that if something happens tonight, I won't wake up and be able to call 911." That absolutely crushed me. He was very delirious by now, and after speaking to the doctor, there was a belief that it was a sign that his brain was now starting to swell. He slept and on Monday I drove Justin over to my parent's house for dinner but Justin could no longer eat. We went home and Courtney came over with her traditional strawberry milkshakes, which was their ritual. On Tuesday, Justin woke up at about 6:00 a.m., and was not feeling well. He looked like he was passing out and now I was really scared. I called Dr. Weil who told me to call 911 and have him rushed over to Mary Washington Hospital in Fredericksburg, so that he could be prepped for an emergency return to Inova Hospital. He had a temperature now of 103 and was so weak, I had to carry him down to the ambulance. Just before we left the house for the ambulance, those last few words from Justin remain locked up inside me. He was really out of it and said, "I almost made it...almost hit a homerun but it landed on the warning track." All I could muster to say was no Justin, you hit a grand slam."* Each and every time Craig and I talked and those last words came up, the pain welling up inside of him was far too much to handle. He broke down once again, and in that one moment of recitation, we all joined him.

Craig also reflected on the last couple weeks of Justin's life. Craig was home with Justin and asked him if he wanted to watch a movie. He said sure and Craig started flipping through channels. As Craig passed by the Nature Channel, Justin asked him to turn it back for a minute. Craig said, *"Justin asked me if I knew what his favorite animal was. I was guessing because he was strong and courageous, it had to be a lion or a tiger. Justin said, "no dad, it's an elephant, because they are so smart and never forget a thing." As Justin looked at me, suddenly tears started running down his face, and he said something that even now breaks my heart. He said "dad, don't ever forget about me." I started crying uncontrollably and told him I would never forget him, and how much I loved him. He just took some deep breaths, paused and said, "dad, please take real good care of Jordie for me." I just reached over and pulled him to me and hugged him tight. I think it was the longest, best hug a father and son could have ever had. But I was dying inside. I was losing my son."*

The saddest part of that story as Justin was being placed into the ambulance, was how Craig described his stricken son make final eye contact, and give his Dad a majestic double thumbs up gesture. Darrell commented about one other thing in one of his last moments with Justin. He couldn't help but to bow his head, cover his eyes and cry. As his pain subsided he said, *"Justin was dying and he was so worried about his father's sadness. The strength in that boy was incredible...so loving, and giving everything he had in this fight right up until the very end."*

As my time wound down with Barb and Darrell, I knew I was nearing the moment when I was to ask a very painful question. I turned and asked Barbara if she recalled her last words with Justin and of her reflections of that time. Barbara, greatly pained and taking her time said, *"I told him the day he died how much I loved him, and whispered to him about what a great kid he was. What I saw next stunned me. As I said that, a single, slow tear ran down his cheek. Oh God, I never told anyone that before."* Barbara broke down crying, and the familiar return of a lump to my throat was heavy and painful, as she recalled Justin's last moments. Barbara went on to say, *"the life support equipment was turned off, but that strong heart of Justin's beat on for close to four hours. That one tear that ran down his face told me right then and there that he heard every word I said."*

I knew Darrell's final thoughts about Justin were next, and I could almost feel the deep heaviness of his heart once again. Darrell said his last words with Justin occurred before he was taken from Mary Washington Hospital to Inova. He leaned in and said, *"I love you grandpa. I have a feeling I may not see you in the morning."* I probably knew that too but that was so hard to hear Justin say that to me. Since that time, I think of Justin's final words *"love you,"* and realized that the number of letters matched Justin's number seven. I think of that all the time. Barbara and I were not just Justin's grandparents. With his death we lost a son."

Following Justin's death on April 7th, Barbara told me that in September, she decided to take a bus tour to Ireland with close friends. She needed a getaway, and she knew that during Justin's illness, she could never be comfortable going anywhere. Barbara said, *"as we were driving, all of a sudden I saw a double rainbow. I had never seen anything so beautiful before, and never two at the same time. I instantly remembered how Justin and I always talked about the beauty of rainbows, and how much he loved them. The whole sky turned into a series of rainbows. It was absolutely incredible. The bus driver told us that he had never seen rainbows like this, and in Ireland he had never even heard of anyone seeing rainbows like this. The more I stared at those rainbows back then, and now, I felt like they were a sign from Justin. I think he did that for me."*

As were ready to say goodbye, I asked Barb and Darrell if they had any final thoughts. I think we all felt the drain of our emotional purge together, and you couldn't help but to feel exhausted. Barbara said, *"you know, in all of my years working in health care, we in the business have to remain so strong and professional all of the time. But I think for most of us who do this work, when you are all alone at night, your emotions must have a way to seep out. With Justin's death, I felt truly crushed and empty. Speaking for Darrell, and all of us for that matter, I don't think we will ever get over losing him. He was just that special."*

As we grabbed our trash and readied to stand up, I felt as if I had known Barbara and Darrell for a lifetime. They epitomized loving, caring grandparents to the very core of their existence. They grieved even now, for the memories of the past remained alive and equally traumatic. I felt I truly had nothing to offer, yet something occurred to me as soon as Barbara had finished talking. Each person who reminisced about time on this earth spent with Justin Whitaker, remarked how he was forever that someone who you could never forget, regardless of time's passage. All of the people offering their love in this book, brought me to only one conclusion. I told Barbara, Darrell, and Craig that their stories only enriched the effervescent memories that we all share. As simplistic as it may sound, all I could offer to them was to say that Justin was not just a student you remembered in the classroom, or a student athlete who excelled and drove himself on a baseball field. I told the Whitakers on that day, that I honestly felt that Justin was a gifted *student of life*…a courageous, loving, caring *student of life*. Even now as I write those words, the tears that welled repeatedly in our eyes as we memorialized Justin in the coffee shop, returned once again. In Justin you truly felt as if you had been touched by an angel.

Lisa's Tears

Lisa Linares came into full focus as a tiny framed girl who was seen wearing a dark dress, as she slowly got out of her chair and walked toward Justin's casket. The sadness felt within the North Stafford gymnasium for Justin's memorial service was immense, yet suddenly, everyone riveted their attention to a diminutive angel carrying one single rose. Lisa Linares loved Justin too, yet there was something so moving, so deeply surreal about this act, that it silenced an entire audience of mourners.

In April of 2006, Lisa was diagnosed with Embryonal Rhabdomyosarcoma, a fast growing, highly malignant tumor which unfortunately, accounts for over half of the soft tissue sarcomas in children. Rhabdomyosarcoma often causes a noticeable lump on a child's body. In Lisa's case, it was a cancerous tumor involving her muscles, and was found to be pushing toward her brain stem. Lisa's type of cancer was the most common found for children under the age of fifteen, and the majority are located in the head and neck areas. The positive thing for this sweet lady, was that Embryonal Rhabdomyosarcoma is considered to be the most treatable form of the disease. Sadly, overall, 50% of children who are diagnosed with this form of cancer, only survive for approximately five years.

Doctors normally treat this cancer through surgical means, generally through chemotherapy, and radiation. Study groups have historically set the stages for treatment from the mildest form as a stage one, to the most severe treatment measures of stage four. In Lisa's case, when she was first diagnosed, doctors felt her tumor was already between stage two and three. Simply because of the size of the tumor, doctors decided to treat Lisa's illness very aggressively, and embarked on the most rigorous, stage four treatment plan. Lisa's mother, Danicela Linares, commented on those first dark days saying, *"at first she received very intensive chemotherapy, and radiation treatments to her head and neck. Doctors told us at first, that there* was a high probability she could lose her right ear as a result, but thank God that didn't happen. During a second biopsy procedure later, doctors again gave me bad news, saying that this biopsy may paralyze Lisa. So basically for the better half of that year, she was in and out of the hospital for treatments. She also had to be treated for running high fevers, and fighting various bacteria issues along the way."

We now flash back in time to the fortuitous meeting between one Justin Whitaker, and the adorable Ms. Lisa Linares at the Inova Fairfax Hospital. Lisa began receiving her treatments at a time when Justin first arrived at Inova. Danicela recalled seeing Justin right away saying, *"I saw Justin, his family and a lot of his friends when he arrived. Shortly after I began meeting the family members, there was one day when Justin's mother Shelia, her sister, and her daughter walked into Lisa's room and asked if I believed in miracles. I told her that I absolutely did, and I remember how convinced Shelia was that Justin would be cured of his cancer, and that everything would turn out fine. What was funny at the time, was that I really didn't know Justin well then, but I immediately got this good impression about him. I watched as his family and good friends gathered, and I knew that he was very special and had such great support through this most difficult time. I think what I felt as I watched Justin's family and friends, was this total sense of shock. I perfectly understood those emotions, because six months before, I was in the same situation when we were first told of Lisa's cancer. I found myself in the role at that time, to try and calm people if they stopped in Lisa's room, because I understood their grief."*

Danicela Linares held great recall about her newfound friend, Justin Whitaker. As described by Craig and Shelia, Danicela spoke of the same loving bond that soon developed between a young man, and a sweet angel facing horrific enemies within their bodies. Danicela said, *"I remember when Justin was first admitted, I took Lisa for a walk because as she said, "she was always looking forward to meeting new people in the neighborhood." Lisa and I walked into Justin's room to say hello. He was there with his girlfriend Courtney. Justin and I talked about Lisa's cancer, and he explained what he was fighting when there was this moment I will never forget. Justin turned to Lisa and said, "Lisa, if you can do it…beat this cancer, then so can I." When I look back on that, I felt that at times it must have been so very difficult for Justin in the ICU. He was a teenager in a pediatric section, and was stunned by being told he had cancer.*

But honestly, I think in ways being surrounded by all those little kids fighting to survive, actually made him stronger."

It was now Lisa's turn to speak of Justin, and how she felt when they first met. Lisa said, *"when I first met Justin I said to myself, this poor kid is suffering badly, just like me. He was so nice to me, it was as if he had known me for a long time. As soon as I saw him and we talked, I knew he was a good person. I remember the time when we walked down the hall and sat down, and I gave him my Barbie doll. I thought that by giving him my doll it would make him smile and feel better. I just wanted to be nice and I thought this present from me made him happy."*

Danicela felt that from that moment on, there was a definable bond that formed between Lisa and Justin. Since that time, Danicela said that *"every time they saw each other after that, there were always long hugs and kisses involved. Justin had given Lisa many gifts as well, and she kept and loved them all. Looking back on those days, whenever I saw Justin, I felt that he was going to beat his cancer and be a survivor. He was a very strong boy. When he went to the appointment with his grandparents and found out that his cancer had returned, I was so hurt for him. My heart literally fell apart because that was the last thing I ever wanted to hear about him. I saw the sadness in his eyes, and I am sure he saw it in mine. I felt so sorry and helpless. Lisa and I speak about Justin all of the time. We choose to think about the good memories we have of him within our hearts. One of those was at the picnic. I can still see Justin now taking pictures with Lisa, and watching them have fun together. We were so glad to see him so healthy, and he was doing great at that time. One other time at a Christmas party, Justin, his family, and friends were giving away teddy bears to all the little kids at the hospital. Justin gave Lisa and her sister Kate one. That was the Justin Whitaker that is in my mind. That was so very nice of him. He was just so special, so very kind, and I am sure that anyone who knew him has nothing but the best of memories spent with him."*

Danicela Linares painted a beautiful picture of Justin Whitaker within the cancer ward at Inova. He was *always* there for *everyone*! Craig would later weigh in on the gift of teddy bears to all the children too. In typical J.W. fashion, he looked around and was immediately worried about everyone else, with nary a worry for himself. Justin soon found out that at the tender age of sixteen, he was the oldest patient in the unit. It was the 'big brother' moving down the halls, "making his rounds" as he used to say. As Christmas was approaching, Craig asked Justin what he wanted. As Craig explained, without hesitation Justin said, *"dad, I would like to buy teddy bears for the kids in the hospital and pass them all out."* Craig explained that there were twenty rooms and an equal number of children. Craig said, *"Walmart had these special edition teddy bears, and they were kind enough to donate half of the cost, while I paid for the other half. You cannot even imagine the excitement as Justin had those bears and was about to give them away. The excitement on the faces of all the children was absolutely priceless. The bears as presents to the children while he was hospitalized, was an idea born from Justin's kindness. When Justin died, Shelia, Jordie, Courtney, Zac, and myself felt that this tradition must continue. It was especially hard having the first Christmas without Justin, but his legacy lives on in that way too now. It was just us now "making the rounds," doing what Justin would have wanted us to do. We intend to be there every Christmas as a way to honor the memories that were all started because of Justin's generous heart and soul."*

Moving back to the Linares family, I knew in my heart how deeply troubled Danicela and Lisa were as they remembered things associated with Justin's eventual death. Yet, there was a warm sense of love and loyalty expressed by them at every turn as they spoke of Justin, his family, and all those who also loved him. Danicela remarked, *"I remember how sick Lisa was when diagnosed with cancer, as her blood counts and immune system dipped lower and lower. Watching how courageous she was fighting her illness, was the same as watching Justin's fight. There was a sense of courage always, and there was never any thoughts about **ever giving up!**"* After Danicela made that comment, I couldn't help but to align Lisa Linares' courage right next to that of Justin's. The "never give up" mantra was professed on so many levels, regardless of the dire circumstances facing him. There was a clear vision of duality when you look at the lives of Lisa Linares and Justin Whitaker. Danicela added, *"I must say that when Justin's fight ended, even though he did not win, I was so very proud of the dignity in which he lived his life, and how he fought to survive. I was so proud of Courtney as well. How she managed to keep her strength over Justin's whole ordeal, and stay with him until that last moment was amazing. I am also so proud to have met his family and friends over all of those hard times. Those days and nights were so depressing, and offered new meaning to the term of suffering. Justin was such a special boy…a fine young man."*

ON THE SEVENTH DAY OF APRIL....SUPERMAN DIED

Danicela and Lisa truly offered a mural image for me about *who* Justin was as that *"fine young man,"* similar in nature to everyone I had spoken to about him, but in a deeply personal way. Pain strikes us all a little harder whenever we witness children suffer, regardless of how it happens. In Lisa Linares, you see this tiny creature inflicted with a silent enemy that so far, she has risen up to conquer. Justin's campaign of war may not have gone as planned, yet in his fight we were witness to something more remarkable. It *did* make us all realize how fleeting life can be, and there truly is no rhyme or reason as to when our time on this earth shall end. But we managed to learn from loss, because Justin made us pay attention. I cannot fathom Lisa's pains as she walked toward the casket during the memorial service, to lay a rose on polished wood and say goodbye to her beloved friend. Danicela and Lisa both ached as they neared closure with me, yet I felt the need to seek out their thoughts when realizing how close Justin was to death. Danicela said, *"Justin lived with love and positivity all around him his entire life. When I learned that he had passed away, I wasn't sure if it would be a good idea to even tell Lisa right away. I was aching inside and was not sure how she would take this terrible news. I knew in my heart that there were two things that were going to deeply affect her. First, she was losing a friend she loved, and second, she knew that his death resulted from cancer. For a little girl, she knew well of the bad things that cancer causes, and she also faced death twice in her own situation. When Justin's mother called me and wanted us to be a part of the memorial service and funeral, she felt it would be nice for Lisa to be there too. I told Lisa that Justin had died, and was so worried how she would react. Lisa simply said, "Mom, I am ready." I was so stunned that she handled such awful news in such a mature way."*

The moment arose once again, as Lisa Linares stood up from her seat amidst a hushed, packed gymnasium, and slowly moved toward Justin's casket. Danicela was scared for her daughter's emotions, yet as Danicela explained, *"she could not wait for that moment when she could walk toward the casket and gently place the rose down. There was something about that moment that was perfect...just the right time."* Lisa commented on this moment as well, something that will be forever etched within her mind. Lisa said, *"I felt like I was going to start to cry, because when I saw Justin in the casket, I knew that this was the saddest day of all. I knew at that moment that I would honor Justin by doing great things for others because I care, and want so much to help people."* Danicela added that, *"we will always remember Justin Whitaker. When he died, Lisa said "Mom, Justin went to heaven. He is going to see God now." I know how Justin's faith pushed him through most of his hard times. I promised Lisa we would go to the cemetery and visit Justin soon. She said that she looked forward to being near her friend again."*

As for Lisa Linares as of March 2009, she continues to be examined very closely every three months, where constant scans and blood count checks are done. She still suffers from the side effects of her chemo treatments. At times, it has been very rough for her to maintain a regular school schedule, as she tries to regain a sense of normalcy in her life. Danicela said, *"I guess the two of us are trying to regain that sense of normalcy. I think because of what she has been through, being a "normal" girl is somewhat difficult for her. To her credit, after such emotional and physical pain, Lisa still remains full of good ideas, and warm intentions to always reach out and help others."* Lisa said, *"I want to help children with cancer and their families who are in need. I would name it the 'Lisa Linares Foundation,' because I want everyone to know that I am with them all the way."* Lisa recently finished her treatments and at the present time, has been in remission for just over a year and a half.

For some odd reason, once again as I finished with Danicela and Lisa, I was struck by something very spiritual…moving. I had a flashback at something from my past, that seemingly tied into emotions aligning with Justin's death. I'm probably dating myself as a baby boomer but, as I finished a section of writing, I suddenly recalled a quote from a 1970's era movie, Brian's Song. The movie was the true story of Brian Piccolo, a running back with the Chicago Bears, who at the age of twenty six, died from cancer. He left behind a loving wife, and three beautiful daughters. For the younger generation flipping these pages, I urge you to watch this movie, yet equally warn you that it is true, very sad, and emotionally charged. Brian's head coach at the time was George Halas, a Hall of Fame legend. In a gut wrenching speech in front of the media, Halas said, *"he left a great many loving friends who miss, and think of him often. But, when they think of him, it's not how he died that they remember…but how he lived. How he did live!"* Justin Whitaker also lived his life in the same ways in which that quote honored a professional athlete who was struck down in the prime of his life. *"How he did live...how he did live!"*

A Best Friend and Comrades Bid Adieu

Four days after Justin had been to Virginia Beach, and given Courtney her promise ring, Zac Briley stood in the quiet, solemn confines of Justin's room within the ICU at Inova Fairfax Hospital in Virginia. It was far too surreal to imagine that his best friend for life, was lying there helpless and comatose, surviving now only through mechanical means. As Zac, Justin's father, and other family members sadly watched the rise and fall of Justin's chest as the ventilator made a rhythmic clicking sound, Courtney entered the room to ask how he was doing. All Craig could manage to say to Courtney was that *"he's dying."* Zac hugged Courtney as they both wept.

Courtney, probably for the first time, was hit with the sudden shock that Justin was *really* slipping away. She could not bear to see one she loved so much, seemingly disappearing before her eyes. She hugged everyone in the room and gently bent over Justin's prone body, kissing him on the forehead, and one last time saying, *"I love you."* To compound the immense pain felt in this cramped room at that very moment, was to look at Zac's sunken expression. It was cruelly ironic that on this seventh day of April, when Justin would pass away, was also Zac's eighteenth birthday. Earlier that morning, Courtney and her school friends had made Zac a birthday cake, with colorful posters to try and cheer him up. By early afternoon, Justin was removed from life support, and for several hours he fought the good fight as he had always done. It didn't seem that long ago for Zac to remember when Justin, in this same ICU ward, spent so much time with other younger cancer patients at Christmas time. Zac remembers Justin giving them stuffed bears to play with, and always making them smile. Now, Zac stared in pain at his best friend who was lying there lifeless and still, aching for a return of those past days of seeing that light of life in Justin's eyes again.

ON THE SEVENTH DAY OF APRIL....SUPERMAN DIED

When Zac and I talked, he reflected back to 7th grade when he first met Justin, when both of them were students at Rodney Thompson Middle School in Stafford, VA. I laughed when I asked Zac when he first talked with Justin, and at what point they became friends? Zac matter-of-factly said that he first met Justin when they were both serving detention time after school. Like cons in prison, Zac smiled and said they each asked the other "what they were in for," as if Rodney Thompson was some medium security prison. Comparing adolescent crimes became the roots for a friendship that bonded immediately. After middle school, Zac like Justin, went to Colonial Forge High School for the first couple months before they both transferred to North Stafford.

Zac recalled the time when Justin first became sick. He developed a lump on the side of his throat, and when he was first brought to the doctor, they felt it was nothing more than mononucleosis, or a cold causing swollen tonsils. Zac also remembered the tough time Justin had when just taking normal breaths. Craig, Justin's dad, thought that to be safe, he would bring Justin to Potomac Hospital in Woodbridge, VA., because the swelling in his neck had also affected his throat. It was at that point where the CT scan revealed that Justin had masses of cancer throughout his chest and lung areas. Zac sadly recalled how Justin was then rushed to Inova Fairfax for emergency care and further tests. Two days later after biopsies were performed, it was determined that Justin had the non-Hodgkin's T-Cell Lymphoma cancer.

That was the very beginning of Justin's fight with cancer, and Zac remembered every moment of it, as if he were watching a movie of what had transpired. Zac said that Justin never spoke of *why* this deadly cancer had taken over his body, and that he was far more aggravated that it may disrupt baseball, and his life in general. Zac spoke in amazement at how strong Justin's demeanor was at the very beginning of it all, and the manner in which he kept handling things when his condition worsened. Zac added, *"there were times when Justin would let his guard down, but would only do it in front of his father, Jordie, Courtney, and me for the most part. There was one time when he looked at me with a sad face and asked why me, and told me how much pain he was in all the time. But for the most part, he just kept things to himself, and never wanted to feel as if he was burdening anyone with complaints."*

In the latter stages, especially after his return from Virginia Beach with Courtney, Zac felt that this would be just another fight that Justin had on his hands. Zac was also shocked at how many of Justin's friends throughout so many years, and across so many school boundaries, came to visit him and later share tears as well. *"I was shocked at the waves of people that came to see Justin on those last couple days. There was no such thing as rival schools anymore. I think each and every person could place themselves in Justin's shoes because of his age. It was just amazing."* Zac then remarked, *"it wasn't at all like I thought it would be. As I watched him lying still in the ICU, all I could remember was how we took college visits together our junior year. Because of Justin's illness, I told him that we could start out going to school on a community college level, because it was close to the doctors and his treatments. I just naturally felt that he would get his strength back, and we would go to school together."* Zac then smiled and said that another thing he remembered clearly, was how much Justin talked about one day being a Marine, and proudly serving his country. *"He was so angry about the whole terrorism thing that he wanted to go over and fight for his country too. There is no doubt in my mind he would have made one hell of a Marine."*

Zac, Courtney, and Justin also talked about her upcoming entry into Hofstra University in the fall, and of playing on the softball team after earning an athletic scholarship. As it related to Courtney, every time I watched her interact with close friends at games, she always had that extra edge that you see and feel in an athlete. It is difficult to define, yet not hard to notice. There was an impenetrable part of her that was strong and mature, yet at times, you could see when pains emanated from within. When Zac and I discussed college, Courtney glanced over with a very sad expression and said, *"my entire college experiences, and all that I do on the field from this point on, will be for Justin. I am very excited to go to college, but right now, it feels bittersweet. I wanted Justin to see me play, and every once in a while glance up and see him there smiling…rooting me on. I wanted him to come to the campus and see where I go to school and meet my friends too. Now I am just very sad that he is gone and won't be with me. It's just not the same."*

Zac remained with Justin the entire time as he gradually watched his best friend drift away. For Zac, it was almost impossible to fathom that Justin would die on the same day he was born. *"When I woke up on April*

ON THE SEVENTH DAY OF APRIL....SUPERMAN DIED

7th, I knew it was my birthday and felt numb and cold. I could only ask how something like this could happen on this day, and what meaning it may hold for me later in life? I wish I could describe what I was feeling but it is impossible," Zac said. Yet, Zac also knew that if these roles were reversed, Justin would have been standing tall at his side, and would never waver. In a later conversation, Zac remarked that in the months following Justin's death, he had a lot of time to reflect on the spiritual, and religious aspects tied to Justin's death. He spent lots of late nights with Justin, long after the 8:00 p.m. visiting hours ended, as nurses allowed him to stay as long as he wanted. Zac said, *"in the darkness of the room I had the chance to be totally alone, and to truly talk to him. Those talks helped me change my views on what the true meaning of life is. I still see him in that room fighting for his life, and in very special, personal ways it has allowed my faith to strengthen. I don't get as sad now, and find more inner peace thinking of all the good times, and years spent as Justin's friend. I visit the cemetery often, and I still have the same type of talks today, as I did when he was alive. If I am down or angry about something, I find serenity there because I know Justin is listening I think we all take far too much for granted as to what we have in our lives, and the special things surrounding us every day. Before Justin became sick, I always thought of cancer happening to someone else, far removed from my world. Today, whenever I hear another story about someone afflicted with cancer, I feel my heart sink because I know how much it affects everyone close to that person. I honestly feel like I suddenly grew up in life because of lessons learned from Justin's death."*

Zac remembered how Justin had difficulty sleeping, and was obviously in pain, but he *never* complained and always remarked that *"everything was going to be all right."* When asked if he ever had any private thoughts about Justin that he would like to share, Zac said that on Justin's last day of life, he asked to be alone with Justin for a few minutes. The doctor told him that Justin could hear his voice, and to feel free to talk with him. Zac spoke of the sadness he felt on the last day of Justin's life, when glancing at Justin lying motionless in bed. Zac said, *"his physical appearance completely changed, and to me it seemed that his being was merely a shell of the person I knew so well. It was so hard to see him that way, and I had to come to terms that he was soon leaving us."* Zac related to me that the talk was *"very personal and between best friends. I knew in my heart that he heard every word. I just knew he did."*

In some ways, Zac and all of Justin's family and friends mourned in special, private ways, yet were able to move on because they inherently understood and adopted Justin's message of *"never giving up...never."* His father Craig said it best when he commented to me that *"he was just one of those rare kids. He inspired all who came across him when he was sick, and throughout all the tough battles that no eighteen year old should ever have to go through. The longer he lived, more people seemed to flock to us in support. So many people...strangers came up to me, or said in notes that because of Justin, it made them better people in general...better husbands or wives, mothers, and fathers to their own children. In Justin I think the entire community came together, and became a little stronger and more bonded as human beings. I think everyone came to understand the truest meanings of life through Justin's death."* The Whitakers and I later discussed this immense support, as they mentioned the Friendship Baptist Church and White Oak Equipment Inc., out of Fredericksurg, Virginia. They raised an incredible amount of money ($32,000) for Justin's cause with their 24th Annual Oyster Roast on March 1, 2008, one thin month away from Justin's death. Over a 23 year period, the generosity of that group totaled over $524,000 in donations for those in critical need. Shelia Whitaker later said, *"we could not imagine that so many people supported Justin out of the pure kindness of their hearts. People just kept coming through the door in waves, and the donation container was literally flowing over. It brought tears to the eyes of all of them. God bless everyone involved who helped us out at such a difficult time."*

The support for Justin did not end there. Along with the Outback restaurant donation of $6500, North Stafford High School raised $20,000, and across town, Colonial Forge raised another $2,000. CiCi's Pizza chipped in with $1000, and the Ladies Auxiliary of the B.P.O.E. (Fredericksburg) donated $500, as did the Stafford Baseball League, where Justin first learned *how* to play the game. The SBL also agreed henceforth, to have an annual scholarship in Justin's name, in the amount of $500. Stafford County, Virginia was a community of giving, considerate souls in the eyes of the Whitakers and everyone that loved Justin. Craig said, *"we will never, ever forget how everyone who helped us out, along with all of the private donations, eased our intense pains. We cannot thank everyone enough."*

Returning to youthful times and friends of the heart, Sean Deasy was a lifelong friend who knew when he first met Justin, that he was someone special. Sean said that he and Justin's friendship went back to elementary school and said that, *"I would describe the two of us forming a brotherhood, rather than a friendship. He had a passion for cars and baseball though, without a doubt. He told me that one day he was going to be a baseball star, and in the same breath he said I would work on all his cars because I was a techie. It is hard for me now to pick out a best memory, because any time spent with Justin was always the best. That is just how he made you feel. When he started to get really sick, I got a tattoo of his initials on my arm, while he stood right beside me watching. That meant a lot to me. I told him, Justin, no matter what happens from here on, we will **always** be brothers. He blew me away all the time. I would always ask him how he was doing, because he was so sick. But, he never answered me and always spun it around asking, "never mind me...what's up with you?" It was a great honor to know Justin, and a big honor to be there with and for his family. Even though sometimes I didn't know what to do when things got really bad, I just tried to do what I could for him and his family. It was just the right thing to do. To be honest with you, I never thought that it was possible that Justin's sickness would take his life. I had always heard about it from others but, not him. After he died, I would sit by myself at night and just stare up at the stars and talk to him. I would dial his cell number too, with the hope that he would always answer, but happy just to hear his voice on the message. Even now, months and months after he died, I still have a lot of trouble accepting it. I was never a good student in school, and to be really honest, I never thought I would be able to graduate. But you know what? I dug in and did it for Justin. I think graduation day was by far, one of the hardest days of my life. I remember as Justin and I were growing up, we always talked about that day, and doing it together with all our friends. As hard as it was that day waiting for my diploma, I still feel that we **did it together!** Today as I think of him, I believe that it has absolutely made me a better person. I feel that I want to help my friends out more, and be there for them when they need me. Most importantly though, losing Justin has showed me that that no matter what conditions surround you in life, you can still have fun and enjoy each day that is given to you, and live your life to the fullest. Justin did! I miss you Justin Lee Whitaker. We will meet again my brother."*

I was moved to a quaking, inner disturbance in taking in Sean's words. They were similar to others, yet vastly different, because I think it dug deep into the core of kindness and considerations given to another human being in time of need. Sean seemed to hit it all without even realizing it. I felt it and was touched by a friend's compassionate memorial.

Returning to one of Justin's baseball comrades, Nate Moore, a baseball player with Justin at North Stafford, talked to me about having a similar background and a bonding that was also born out of an illness. Nate first attended Brooke Point High School, and transferred to Wolverine land his sophomore year. He first met Justin as they took to the baseball field at North, and they became workout partners and friends. Nate told Justin that he suffered from diabetes, and it seemed that when Justin was first diagnosed with cancer, the two became far more than just players on a diamond. Nate said, *"it was funny in a way because he knew I had diabetes, and when Justin first learned of my illness, we became instantly closer. He would always joke with me about my sugar levels, and the amazing thing to me was that he seemed far more concerned with me than he was with his own battles. We would hit the weights and train, and at one point we joked that we were now the 'Mini Men Brothers."*

Nate recalled the day when Coach Labrusciano walked up and told the baseball team that Justin had taken a bad turn, and that everyone needed to prepare for the worst. Nate remembered the coach saying that *"Justin might not make it boys,"* and there was something so strange and almost hard to believe, that it struck everyone very hard. Nate said that between the coaches and seniors, there was a rallying point in it all, and according to him, *"Justin became the glue that held together the North Stafford baseball team. You would think the team would tighten up, but everyone played the game of baseball in the way Justin always did…competitive, but in a fun way. His illness made us all realize that it was truly a game."*

As Justin's condition worsened, Nate told me that he kept reflecting on words that Justin had said, even in the worst of times that would somehow boost his own spirits. There was one occasion when they talked about his cancer, and Justin said, *"if this thing goes really bad on me, and if it eventually kills me, I suppose I will be better off and not suffering anymore."*

ON THE SEVENTH DAY OF APRIL....SUPERMAN DIED

Nate's comments compared to Zac's in many regards, because virtually nobody ever spoke of Justin ever giving in to his illness. He fought it at every turn. Nate believes that Justin was merely speaking of facing the realities tied to his cancer, and *if* it were to win, then so be it. Nate saw that at times, Justin's energy would wane, but he always remained upbeat about things, and find something positive to lean on. To Nate, *"there was never a healthy Justin, and a Justin stricken with cancer. There was just 'Justin' and somehow, in some way, you just felt that he would beat his cancer."*

As Nate and I talked about his emotions almost four months after Justin's death, you could feel the pains still clearly emanating from his heart. Yet, he also paused to speak of a deeper inner faith that served as a guide for him whenever he missed Justin's presence. *"I feel at peace now with Justin's death, because I know that one day I would be seeing him again. I also knew that Justin had been saved, and my own faith in Jesus has allowed me peace and strength in a way I never thought was possible, and to move on in my life. Justin Whitaker has bolstered that strength inside of me. I think of him always, and wonder about what his deepest dreams were. I wonder what his life would have been like if he had fought his way through all of this. I know he watched as our baseball team meshed together as one. Through the grace of God we made it through the entire season, and I am convinced it was because Justin was there the entire time. We all talked about what he was doing now as we played the game he loved, but we were all unified in saying that he was absolutely watching over all of us. I think once we all got through the pains of losing Justin on earth, we were able to realize that once you speak of eternity, how much can really affect you? We will all get the chance to see Justin again one day. I have no doubt about that."*

For Mike Wolf, in the summer of 2008, he was preparing to enter his senior year at cross town rival, Colonial Forge High School. Justin attended Forge for one thin term before transferring to North Stafford, yet Mike and Justin had forged their friendship from long ago. They both attended Park Ridge Elementary and like Nate, Mike and Justin met on a ball field. Like most who have spoken about how Justin Whitaker brightened their lives through a mere smile or devilish grin, Mike said that there *"was just always something about Justin that made people gravitate to him. I was amazed that regardless of the setting, whenever anyone met Justin for the first time, it was never a quick hello and goodbye. You tended to stay and talk a while because of the ease and comfort you felt from him."* Mike went on to say, *"as Justin's condition worsened, I can honestly say that he turned into a role model for me. When he was diagnosed with cancer, and I watched first hand how he battled and fought at every turn to live, I felt like my own life and goals began to take shape. I feel now, four months after his death, that as a result of lessons learned from him, I wish to conquer things in life in the same ways in which he battled his illness."*

Talking with Mike, Zac, and Nate all together on a cool morning, they all agreed that Justin's Superman moniker was so appropriate, for so many reasons. Mike spoke for the guys by saying that *"Justin put his own individualized stamp on what Superman was to those seeking to hope for the best. It was that same hope that brought out the Superman character in Justin. He would be hooked to machines with wires and tubes attached to his body everywhere, and you would think that he would be down in the dumps and out of it. Not Justin! He would start smirking, and do these Rocky Balboa lines like he was a fighter in the ring who could take every punch and still come at you. There was one time I remember well when ICU nurses were going to give him two shots at the same time in each leg. Justin just grinned and said, "come on, give me more. I can take it." That was just the way he was. Superman took punch after punch until he couldn't take them anymore."*

When Mike was asked about the amazing community support for Justin at every turn, he too remains stunned that Justin's story touched the deepest core of people living virtually everywhere. Mike proudly said that *"once Justin died, everyone, and I mean everyone, came together as family. There were no more school enemies or boundaries, and the common theme was that everyone shared this abundance of love for Justin. To this day people from all over the state and beyond, see our bracelets, our tattoos, and even if these people are strangers, we talk about Justin and keep his spirit alive. It's easier for me now to accept the religious aspects of Justin's death. Justin was saved, and as a Christian, he knew that he was soon going to be in a better place. For me, and those closest to Justin, accepting the reality of his impending death made it that much more acceptable. He would finally suffer no more pain, and his soul would be at ease."*

As were about to finish our morning chat, Zac, Nate, and Mike talked collectively about no longer feeling as lost teenagers, but as men who had been taught valuable life lessons. Their individual maturation processes had been accelerated by Justin's illness, and subsequent passing. Speaking for the group, Mike simply said, *"Justin's death made us all grow up. I believe I speak for his family, friends, and all around Justin who after his death, felt this immense wave of change rising from within. I used to complain about everything...life in general. Now when saddled with work duties, chores, or depressing times, I choose to think of the ways in which Justin marched on and answered challenge after challenge without wincing."* In the following one to two months after Justin's death, Zac Briley talked about others in the Stafford County area whose lives were also affected by cancer. One person was a nearby James Monroe High School student, who was ironically diagnosed with a similar lymphoma. Another young girl, who was the sister of one of Justin's best friends, was also diagnosed with thyroid cancer. Mike Wolf again spoke for his buddies by saying, *"I had always heard stories about others affected by cancer, yet it was never a personal thing until it hit home with someone you personally know and love. All I know is that whoever knew or met Justin Whitaker, were gifted by his presence. Now that Justin is gone, all of us* (gesturing to Nate and Zac) *have taken a vow to keep Justin's spirit alive by moving forward with Justin's fund, and making everyone aware that it* **can** *happen to anyone."*

As we were about to say goodbye, I asked the boys if they sought to speak of anything deeply personal about times shared with their buddy Justin in his final days. Nate Moore forlornly said, *"I think we all have private thoughts that we wish to remain private, but we did have the chance to say goodbye alone with Justin, each in our own way. We all had our own time to whisper prayers that I know Justin heard. Even today we all regularly visit the cemetery, and those times alone brings you back to earth. There is peace there that enables you to flush your soul out. There is no doubt that Justin is at rest now, and there is equally no doubt that he left a mark on everyone here."*

One Life to Live

When I met with Craig Whitaker, Courtney Crews, and Zac Briley at a coffee shop to discuss this book for the very first time, I told them that since Justin's death, I have been overwhelmed in many regards. I cannot possibly explain *why*, nor do I seek to make sense of the mystical ways in which I felt driven to honor his life. My entire professional law enforcement career, often times, has dealt with the worst of the worst, and in seeing the more sinister side of life. I suppose most in this profession can relate to the fact that you *do* internalize darkness, yet somehow, you find ways to place it in the far recesses of your mind. As it relates to Justin, there have been emotions raised that made me at least try to take pen to paper each day, and accomplish that which I feel driven to do. Maybe in some humorous, twisted way, I see Justin with that grin, his hat spun around backwards, guiding me with his mantra of *"never giving up."* Along this journey, I found so many things that aligned with his life, and in turn, I have come to understand how it affected all of those touched by Justin's gentle, loving persona.

One day while reading and writing, I re-read something that I had saved over four years ago. In almost an unexplainable, yet spiritual way, it occurred to me *why* I may have saved something that deeply moved me so many years ago. The italicized section below was written by Matthew D. Lazarra, who succumbed to cancer on February 15, 2004. Matthew was only 21 years old, and was from Illinois. Among his many passions, Matthew loved history, and he was a devout Civil War buff. As soon as I read that, I remembered Darrell Whitaker, and Steve Crews telling me at separate times of Justin's love of history, and especially the Civil War. In a poignant note to the Chicago Tribune that was posted on February 19, 2004, Matthew's father Scott said, *"I'd always hoped Matt would live long enough to change the world, even if it was just a little at a time. He had such a good head and heart."* Another young child lost to us forever, without the chance to make a mark in life. The words of Matthew Lazarra to me, were simply amazing when I first read them, and so pointedly appropriate to the emotions coursing through all of us after losing Justin Whitaker.

Matthew Lazarra wrote;

I don't think a lot of people sit around and contemplate their lives. People think about their futures, what they're going to do, and what they should have done in order to achieve something. But, I don't think most people contemplate events unfolding in their present lives. What are you doing right this minute? Everyone understands the premise of living for the moment. Very few though, take actions on things requiring change, myself included. That is something from my past that I have done at times, often falling in deep regret. It is my intention now to guide my future, beginning where I choose to stand today.

Life is a finite thing. There is unspoken realization that at some point, our lives are to end. Mine has a time limit. No surprises for me, and depressingly enough, that 'time' is going to run out rather soon. I've never really told anyone how long I have left, or what exactly (in great detail) is wrong with me, because I would rather my friends view me as a vital, volatile, rather silly human being. At age 21, most people don't understand, or know how to contemplate the thought that someone you know will leave. They would abandon me for more secure, lasting relationships. So every day, each minute…is vital to me. The most mundane things are breaths of fresh air. The things that most people take for granted but shouldn't…a kiss, a pudding fight, a good long walk, or an intriguing conversation, are now intensely important to me. I think they should be important to everyone. The fact that I know I won't be able to experience these things makes them achingly more vital, for they make me desperate to achieve them one more time.

I want to close my eyes and kiss a girl one more time…the kind of kiss that makes you feel like you're floating, where you forget to do something with your hands because it's so good. I want to go camping, and lie in the grass, and think how naively beautiful the day is. I want to shoot off fireworks and run away when the cops pull up. I want someone to hold my hand and tell me something nice about myself. I want to sit on a stoop late into the night, drinking cheap beer, and telling stories. I want to feel alive, not dead or dying, and think that those things, the most trivial and passing connections to the world, the people in it…are vitally important.

So this is my contribution to you. I'm desperately telling all of you to take advantage of your youth and vitality. I hear too many people talking about college and getting their first jobs afterward. I hear too many people talking about work, and how this and that sucks. In reality, we're all wasting our lives doing things that disconnect us from everyone else! You don't need a four or five year plan, and you sure as hell don't need to worry about feeling innocent and immature again. Worry about making every passing day something to talk about, and not just another blank page in your life.

I used to act like you. I had a plan. I had a future and all that blew away, but right now, I barely have life itself and that's how I've realized the error of all our ways. Please…please, don't get old and simply die, or lay here like me suffering from cancer, and realize you did nothing with your life. Make plans in your life that have never happened because you never had the time or drive to accomplish them. Don't miss opportunities anymore. If you like someone tell them. If you think the time is right to kiss someone, do it. If you feel like you're in a rut, do something carefree and silly and just have fun. If you feel the world is ugly, make something beautiful. Stop being so damn cautious! An old movie line I remember is, "if you take life too seriously, you'll never get out alive."

Trust me, as much as life sucks sometimes, it is still the only thing we have that we can change. It is the only thing that matters, and it's wonderful. Life can be a beautiful, ridiculous, tragic disaster, but it's the only thing we have. So don't let it lie by the wayside in pursuit of crap that's barely important. People are the most important resource, and so are the relationships we build with them. I feel the pinch of that more than ever now. If we could spend 400 billion dollars to cure cancer, instead of building, and maintaining weapons, I wouldn't have to write this. So this is, essentially a plea. This is the most personal thing I've ever written, and I hope it reaches more people than I ever could. Tell yourself over and over that this is the only life you have. Make something worthwhile out of it, and no one who you've laughed, cried, kissed, and bled with, will ever forget you…ever!

As I slowly read the words of Matthew Lazarra once again, I felt more power and emotion to his words than ever. In many ways they mirror Justin's urgings before he passed away, in that he told so many not to worry about him, and chose to ask how *their* lives were going. Because Justin and Matthew fully realized that their illnesses may take them from this earth, without a doubt, I feel that nothing they imparted to anyone was ever accidental. Amidst saddened, facial expressions, or through soft, spoken words, we have experienced the dreadful tragedies tied to life's passing, and placed ourselves in the shoes of those taken from us. As Matthew Lazzara so poignantly expressed, *"this is the only life you have."* We learned through our time in knowing Justin Whitaker, that Matthew's words are undoubtedly true. Because of that, all of our lessons learned in life and ultimately in death, will *never* be forgotten.

The Silent Grief of Caregivers

A Nurse's Prayer

Give me strength and wisdom,
When others need my touch;
A soothing word to speak to them,
Their hearts yearn for so much.
Give me joy and laughter,
To lift a weary soul;
Pour in me compassion,
To make the broken whole.
Give me gentle, healing hands,
For those left in my care;
A blessing to those who need me,
This is a Nurse's prayer.

Allison Chambers Coxsey
c1997

I looked at numerous poems about nursing and care giving, yet nothing seemed to touch the poignancy within the prose of Ms. Coxsey. Her words correlated perfectly to the thorough, professional, medical attention rendered to Justin and his family at every turn. So many warm, kind words were echoed by everyone about his exceptional care, because in many ways, akin to how Justin lived his own life, nurses and doctors always seemed to go that extra mile. They understood Justin's fight, and chose to dig in with him, regardless of the dire circumstances surrounding their mission.

Dr. Marcie Weil, by all accounts, epitomized the dedication to one's mission, while performing a delicate balancing act of making sure that the patient being treated, was *still* a person to be compassionately dealt with. Each and every person I have spoken to over this past year, when discussing issues tied to Justin's medical care, *always* added the name of Dr. Weil to the conversation during critical, painful times. Dr. Marcie K. Weil, a physician specializing in Pediatric Hematology-Oncology, was Justin Whitaker's savior for a time at Fairfax Inova, and by all accounts, an angel for all of eternity. Dr. Weil remarked that she recalled clearly the first time she met Justin. She said, *"I met Justin in the Intensive Care Unit, while he was awake and we were preparing to begin a biopsy of his tumor. He had too much disease in his chest to lie flat and be sedated for the procedure. My first impression was how handsome he was, and that he looked like a teenaged athlete. My second thought was how brave he was to be doing this procedure while awake. He was given medicine to reduce his anxiety. I also had to do a bone marrow test on him at the same time, which is a painful procedure. I did give him some medicine to take the edge off, because usually we have patients sleeping through this procedure. His bones were very hard, so the procedure proved to be more difficult than usual. I commented to Justin about how hard his bones were, and he turned and told me, "I'm the Man of Steel." Coincidentally, he had Superman boxers on. We all laughed so much during the procedure, and periodically whenever we recall that comment. Justin had gone to an event with Courtney at some point dressed as Superman. His friends and family acknowledged him as Superman. He* **was** *a super man! He was an amazing person."*

Marcie shed more light on Justin's deadly disease, and commented on many facts related to Justin's T-Cell lymphoma. Dr. Weil said, *"Justin was treated for T-Cell according to standard T-Cell therapy. His tumor regressed quickly. I remember showing his family x-rays pointing out how quickly the tumor was shrinking. Justin experienced a great deal of pain in his knees as a result of the chemotherapy. Relatively early in his therapy, Justin developed a condition known as osteonecrosis, which is de-vitalization of the bone secondary to decreased blood flow. That is a side effect of steroids. Baseball was Justin's passion. But, a side effect meant that Justin would not have been able to play baseball professionally in the future if he survived his illness. Knowing he had osteonecrosis, Justin never asked me whether he would be able to play. I don't know if he did not want to know the answer, or if he knew that surviving his cancer with all the side effects that might result, was our primary goal. It also crossed my mind that he did not want others to know that he would never play baseball professionally. Justin was very protective of his family. He did try and play baseball whenever possible, despite the pain he was going through. I know that he had a love of the game, and the friends he played it with. I asked him toward the end of his life, what things he wanted to get done. He answered, "one last game of baseball, to go on a trip with my family, and give the ring to Courtney. It was in that one conversation that he told me that he had faith that God would take care of him no matter what happened."*

Justin's spirit came into sharp focus with Dr. Weil, as she watched a young man desperately fight his illness. Marcie said, *"Justin had a very kind, gentle spirit. He never once came into the office talking about himself. He almost never complained. He was frequently in pain, but either family members would pass that information on to us, or we would have to ask him. He was so humble as well. He never bragged about himself either. A good example about that was when his father had to tell me that Justin had been inducted into the Baseball Hall of Fame. Yet, Justin never wasted a moment bragging about Courtney's play in softball. He was both fun and funny. He was so determined, whether it was playing baseball when in extreme pain, flying to Florida when he was coming close to the end of his life, or giving Courtney the ring on the beach at sundown, on his very last day outside the hospital."*

Clearly though, Dr. Weil was very much aware about the mark that Justin left behind on other patients suffering from cancer at Inova. Marcie remarked that, *"Justin was so inspirational for other patients. He would play soccer in the hallway with the little boys, and make visitations to other patients in their rooms, telling them not to worry, and that everything would be alright. You could easily see the admiration that other patients had for Justin, because he was a great example and role model for all of them. Justin accepted a Barbie doll from a young, female patient* (Lisa Linares) *who thought that it would be the ultimate gift to give someone she cared for so very much. I never even learned of this until much later. I can say that we all loved and admired Justin just as much as everyone around him that truly knew him. Justin Whitaker taught us all to live life to the fullest, and make every single moment count. He also taught us how to give to others, rather than to bring attention to ourselves. A good example of that was when communities had events to recognize his plight, Justin never changed. Craig would tell me about the events, or he would tell Justin to pass on what the communities had done in his honor. Justin always seemed a little shy about telling me those things, but never hesitated to comment to me about how nice all the people were for doing what they did for him."*

With all of the heartfelt feelings expressed by Marcie Weil, I had yet to truly tap the deepest emotions from deep within, that she sought now to share as it related to Justin's family and friends. Marcie never missed a beat recognizing each and every person she came in contact with during Justin's long, arduous ordeal. Dr. Weil said, *"I want to convey how much everyone surrounding Justin loved him so much. They were so devoted to him, yet they each expressed their love and affections in different ways, and directed all that they had within their hearts toward Justin. I wanted to say something to each of them…*

To Barbara and Darrell: You invited Justin to stay with you for parts of every week. You brought Justin to most of his appointments. Barbara was one of the first Physician Assistant's that I held knowledge of, so she proved to be of great help to the medical team, in addition to being Justin's loving grandmother. Darrell always brought with him a sense of control and calmness to any situation. I understood over time that he learned to deal with inner turmoil when serving as an Air Force pilot. (Darrell was a decorated full bird Colonel who had extensive time in combat during the Vietnam war). *I am sure that Justin received a great deal of his humility from Darrell, who allowed Barbara to brag about him, because he would never brag about himself.*

To Craig: You had to juggle a demanding job, all the while caring for Justin. Eventually you cast your job aside and devoted yourself to your son. You have done such an incredible job keeping Justin's memory alive for all of us who knew him, and encouraging those who did not know him…to know him now.

To Shelia: Justin felt extremely close to you, even though there may have times when Justin did not see you as much as he would have liked. You offered great spiritual strength and serenity to him at every turn.

To Amber: I watched as you sat at Justin's bedside frequently. I know that you and Justin were incredibly supportive of each other for a lifetime.

To Jordy: You were so very quiet around me in the beginning. I always wondered how hard the whole experience of Justin's illness, and seeing him hospitalized so often was for you. I know that you and Justin were very close friends, as well as loving brothers. I was also worried that all of the attention on Justin, might detract from the attention on you. That is what I have seen with siblings when one is very ill, but more so with you, when so much focus was on Justin. You were far less shy with me toward the end. I was happy that in your own way you were thriving, despite this dreadful experience.

To Shelia's Parents: I watched you sit in Justin's room during his diagnosis, and during his transplant. This was despite Grandpa's blindness, and dealing with his own illness. Grandma also needed to care each day for Grandpa. You came from a long distance away to be by Justin's side.

To Aunt Dee Dee: You were constantly at Justin's bedside in the hospital. This was all the while caring for your own parents when they were at home. I viewed you and Amber as second mothers to Justin. As you and Shelia sang at the memorial, I felt your incredible voices…your deepest inspirations.

To Courtney: I know that you came to the hospital every chance you could. Sometimes, I would look in and see you lying in bed with Justin watching television. We all knew that was not allowed, yet it seemed the proper thing to do in looking the other way. You and Justin were ever so courteous always. You and Justin cared for each other in a very mature way. You loved your sports and played them hard, yet when you dressed for the prom, you looked beautiful. Justin was not only your boyfriend…but your best friend. Justin was so very proud of you for your athletics, and for your academic abilities. I know that he wanted to marry you too. You rallied all of your friends, and an entire school around Justin. You had t-shirts made when Justin returned to school after the initial phase of chemotherapy. At the end of his life, you honored Justin again, with a moving, candlelight vigil.

To Zac: You came to visit your best friend in the hospital whenever you could. Justin was not just a 'friend.' He was a brother to you. In my experiences, I have rarely seen male friendships become so dedicated and strong, as you were with Justin throughout his illness.

To Courtney's Parents: You were so supportive of Justin. Justin confided very personal feelings to Courtney's dad, who would spend many nights with Justin in the hospital. Both of you were equally responsible for insuring that Justin's dying wish would be granted, and he would lovingly offer Courtney her 'Promise Ring.' As that beautiful story was told to me, Courtney looked at both of you standing a short distance away, allowing for their privacy. She stared in your direction and sought your approval with the nod of your heads, so that she knew that it was alright for Justin to make this loving offer. I can't even imagine how confusing it was for your daughter, loving Justin so very much, but equally knowing that he was dying. Those kind of moments only happen in movies, yet there it was before your eyes in real life.

To All of Justin's Loving Friends: I will never in my life forget all of you, crowded into Justin's Pediatric Intensive Care room as he lay still and dying. I have never seen anything like that before, or since. At one point I remember twenty or so of you, encircling Justin's bed. There was music filling the room of all types, from pop, gospel, to the most inspirational. I saw some of you text messaging, and at first I was somewhat taken aback that you were doing it at a time like this. Then another side of me thought you may have been letting others know who could not be there what was happening, and that Justin had little time left to live. While all of this was going on, I said to myself, this is 'Justin's World.' I am so glad that all of you were there supporting each other, and caring for Justin and his family to the very end. I was amazed at how many of you honored Justin with your tattoos sporting Justin's initials. That was your way of remembrance. The acronym of tribute toward Justin of 'What Would Justin Do,' was absolutely perfect and fitting."

After I read and wrote Dr. Weil's open letter tributes and recall of so many people enveloping Justin's life, I truly felt her remarkable, selfless persona. Too many times when all of us deal with health professionals on Dr. Weil's level, we are often left to feel as discarded…waiting for our number to be called for service. Clearly, this was not Dr. Weil, nor anyone associated with the phenomenal care rendered to Justin Whitaker. As Dr. Weil wound down with her most moving summation, we touched upon the subject of her speaking role at Justin's memorial service. Before we bridged that, we touched on the hardships with health professionals dealing with cancer cases, and the worst of the worst. Dr. Weil remarked that, "dealing with adolescent cancer patients is very rewarding, in that you can develop a relationship with them as individuals, rather than through their parents.

ON THE SEVENTH DAY OF APRIL...SUPERMAN DIED

Adolescents going through cancer, are both reflective, and introspective. They have a lot to teach us about life and appreciation. Adolescents though, know the meaning of loss and dying, as opposed to younger children who place all of their trust within their parents, and therefore have less fear of the entire 'dying process.' Taking care of teenagers is most rewarding, yet equally painful. I cope with the death of patients that I become close to, in ways that I know will keep them alive in my heart. That way I can remember all of them frequently with happy memories. I will treasure all that I came to know, and understand about the life of Justin Whitaker. He was an amazing person who taught me about life, humility, encouragement, and spiritual strength. I am thankful to have been invited into his world. I am blessed for his family who openly shared his life with me. Many of my own friends and family who never met or knew of Justin personally, know him now through me and fully understand what a special person he was."

I felt exhausted and emotional as I internalized Dr. Weil's deepest revelations about Justin. The final question entailed by far, the hardest one of all. I sought to know of something personal she may want to share about Justin, yet having it entail something she had yet to discuss. Marcie said, *"sitting myself down to offer words about Justin was very hard for me to do. Life is forever busy, and trying to stop your life and express your feelings is far from easy. Sometimes as you try to 'not' forget about anything as you stop in reflection, provokes great anxiety. Once I started to write things down, my emotions came pouring out. Although I frequently have flashbacks thinking about good memories shared with Justin, it was a good thing to sit and bring back all of those moments again. As I finalized my thoughts, I noticed that it was close to midnight. I made all of my notes at the hospital. Every moment with Justin was worth it. My hope is that everyone reading of Justin now, will get to know him in all the ways that I did. To feel him as you read of his life, is to enrich your own lives, in ways that he touched all of ours."*

One of those closest to Justin during his initial entry into Inova, was Holly Senn. Holly is a Certified Child Life Specialist within the Pediatric Hematology/Oncology unit there. Holly related to me that she met Justin on the very first day he was admitted to the unit. She spent a full day with Justin and his family, and basically went over the varied procedures that he would face along the way. Holly also explained that many of the medical steps in combating his cancer, would have to be accomplished without the use of sedation medications because of the large mass in his chest. Holly clearly held the role as a precarious juggler at times, speaking of extreme measures that were necessary, while equally helping Justin and loved ones with specialized coping mechanisms. Her job was to also try and instill a little fun in her daily work with patients, and clearly the affable Mr. Whitaker enjoyed that as well. Holly described Justin as *"extremely inquisitive, yet anxious,"* as he listened and leaned on all for support. Without Holly even mentioning it, I knew the Justin she was speaking about very well. As a driven young man in school and sports, there was never an obstacle too high, or a goal too far out of reach. Holly aligned that with his own questions as he dealt with his Lymphoma. He was fearful, anxious, and at times angry over the uncertainties before him. Yet she too, felt his raw determination *never* to let anything hinder the path he sought toward recovery. Holly Senn, whom the Whitaker family, Courtney, Zac, and all his loved ones explained to me prior, was a woman with a *"heart of gold."* The more Holly went on to speak of Justin Whitaker, it was clear that she was indeed a rare breed of a person.

In Holly's words, you sensed immediately of an undeniable impact made upon her by Justin. He had that way about him that seemed to provoke deep emotions within anyone spending any appreciable time in his presence. Holly described Justin's fight and demeanor as a *"no fear...whatever it takes"* attitude. There was focus beyond his years as he spoke to Holly of life, school, baseball, college, and where his later years in life may lead him. Akin to how beloved family members spoke of Justin, Holly felt an intense loyalty and love about Justin. It was one in which, regardless of how he was physically or emotionally feeling, he placed others before him always. The uniqueness of Justin Whitaker began to take shape before her eyes as he sought to know of the condition of other patients, while asking the nurses individually how their lives were going. Holly said he knew the nurses by their first names, and whenever he heard that a particular patient may be having a rough time, he was the first to ask if there was something *he could do* to make their world a little brighter. On many occasions, Holly noticed that Justin's attitude alone, often brought out positive emotions and interactions from nurses witnessing his demeanor. Holly added, *"I know that he has forever impacted the care that I provide on a daily basis."*

Realizing that it may invoke sad sentiments within Holly, I felt obligated to ask her of any recollections she may have of Justin's affections for other younger children afflicted with cancer. I specifically asked about *Lisa* who so many have mentioned as being so close to Justin's heart. Holly said, *"I do remember his overwhelming concern for the younger children on the unit who were facing the same, or similar treatments as Justin. Justin's biggest concern was that they were so young, and may not be able to understand or comprehend the situation, and therefore, not cope with things as well. I noticed a relationship between Justin and Lisa that was truly special, touching both of their hearts. Every single time Lisa would see Justin in the hallway, she would smile and she loved it when he spent time in her room and played with her. A lot of times, having a new face brings some excitement to younger children when they want to play, but somehow knowing that this person wanted to be there took it to a higher level. Lisa loved Justin very much, and was so very sad when he died. She attended the memorial service at North Stafford, but at one point I believe she had to leave because she was overcome with grief. I know that Justin has also forever impacted Lisa, and the lives of her family in an immensely positive way that may never be put into words."*

In certain ways, without drawing an analogy to a super hero, Holly Senn *was* indeed placing Justin on the same pedestal as the Superman he was so aptly aligned with. Holly remarked that *"Justin was truly a one of a kind guy. His overall demeanor of compassion, sincerity, humor, athletic ability, intelligence, futuristic dreaming, generosity, and especially his selflessness, made him into something that was indescribable. To be referred to as anyone's Superman was more than fitting."* As so many had commented on before, Holly too held amazement at the countless number of adolescent visitors Justin had. What was so unique to her centered on the fact that Justin was a North Stafford Wolverine ballplayer, and so many others in support of their friend, wore other team jerseys, and once on the playing field, all were fierce opponents. Holly placed her view of competition and compassion within a unique, framed view. She said, *"most of the time, all you ever hear in sports deals with hating other players because of their skill levels. Justin was a good baseball player in one school, but his roots of friendship ran deep, with friends occupying roster spots on "enemy" teams. In Justin, you always had the sense that he put all of that aside, and he truly wanted, and maintained friendships with everyone regardless of who they played for. That is just the way he was. I remember seeing people come to visit him in the hospital, with each having varied lifestyles, but that never came out whenever Justin was concerned. As 'Superman,' he looked at the bigger picture and held an appreciation for all of his friends, because they also had different skills, talents, and interests. He realized the strengths in each person, and as a result, cultivated that relationship."*

If the subject of Justin's friends resonated within Holly's remembrance of Justin, the emotions she still possessed about time spent with Courtney and all family members, was truly something palpable. Holly recalled Justin's grandparents as being at the hospital on most days, and when Justin was sent home, their Fairfax to Stafford, Virginia runs were often five day a week ventures. Holly expressed the fact that Justin's relationship with all family members was beyond close. Holly added, *"Justin's mom Shelia was with him the majority of time during his very first admission, and was always there. She would also stay at night and wake up very early in the morning to get ready for work. Justin's sister, and brother were there often as well and were so very close to him. Justin's dad Craig, came to see Justin at night after work and would bring him dinner, and then hang out with him. The weekends were no different. But of all my memories, I must say that Justin's relationship with his girlfriend Courtney astonished me. I was in awe of their true love and respect for each other despite of their young age. Courtney was always right by Justin's side in the hospital, or on the phone with him when dealing with critical issues of care or concern. I can still hear Justin's voice insisting that Courtney continue on with her regular softball practices and games, regardless of what he was going through. They had a great relationship in so many regards, one that was forever open, loving, supportive, extremely genuine, and at varied times…humorous. To this day as I reflect upon Courtney's selfless sense of fortitude and strength, I know it will be something that always stays with me. She seldomly cried in Justin's presence, and at times it mirrored how a mother may act in protection of her child. As a result of my countless conversations with Courtney, it was natural for us to become closer in spirit. I learned about her love for Justin that will forever remain deeply engrained within my heart."*

ON THE SEVENTH DAY OF APRIL....SUPERMAN DIED

As Holly neared finalization of her thoughts about Justin, it was quite evident that when reflecting on his passing, her personal pains remained raw. It was as if we were dealing with an open wound of sorts. Holly forlornly spoke of her professional role at the hospital in terms that made me feel her heart. She said, *"it has always been my philosophy that I was in a position to support family members as a beloved child is about to die. A secondary emotion became quite evident though, as I truly wanted grieving family members to know that I was by their sides, and that I honestly cared for their child, and all of the pains they were going through. When Justin was slowly passing away, I felt as if I was losing a little brother. Since the very first day we met, we seemingly shared so many common threads. We both held similar attitudes towards life in general, and in those emotions alone, we shared an instant connection. I remember when Justin relapsed and how difficult it was for me. I had a good cry and talked with my mom about how hard my job can be at times. We are trained to not get attached to patients, and to observe boundaries, but sometimes as human beings, there are certain things we have no control over. I definitely felt that time spent with Justin and his family through the worst of times, were events that tested your inner soul. Justin and I would talk about baseball all the time, and one day, he told me how he had been inducted into the Little League Hall of Fame in Cooperstown. He handed me a baseball card of him that was sealed in a plastic case. Right after that conversation Justin said, "hang on to this. It will be worth a lot of money one day." That baseball card to this day, sits on the very top of my refrigerator, so that each and every day I have the feeling he is always looking out for, and watching over me. Justin will never leave my heart."*

As we were finishing things up, I asked Holly if in some small way, she still feels Justin's heart beating within those working such tragic cases of sick children at Inova Fairfax Hospital. Holly sadly said, *"Justin remains the topic of discussion within the ICU from time to time, as well as in my own personal life. I don't think someone like that can ever be forgotten. Justin's spirit was, and still is contagious. One of my fondest memories I hold of Justin, was when I was called to the room of a seven year old boy. As soon as I walked into the room, I was attacked with Nerf darts from every direction from both the young patient, and of course…Justin. Go figure, it was Justin's idea!"*

Just when I thought that I could not become more overwhelmed after taking in Holly's words, I started to go over information provided by Kelly Printz, Justin's *main* nurse. I emphasized the main nurse theme because Kelly always laughed with Whitaker family members about not being able to remember exactly *when* she first began caring for Justin. As Kelly explained, *"there were other nurses that took care of Justin during his initial diagnosis, and I hardly knew who he was. The family, and those closest to Justin, always remarked that it was Justin himself who found me, and that's how I started caring for him. One thing I* **do** *know, is that from the first day I cared for him, right up until the point of his passing, no one else primarily cared for him. Whenever he came into our office, all of the office personnel, nurses, and doctors knew that I would be taking care of him. Even if other patients came in before him, it never altered my care of him personally. I can also say that Justin did his fair share of letting everyone know who was* **his** *nurse as well."*

Kelly went on to say that from the very beginning, she held a close relationship to Justin's grandparents, Darrell and Barbara. They primarily brought Justin to most, if not all of his appointments. Kelly added that *"the relationship I was able to witness between Justin and his grandparents, was beautiful and deeply inspirational. I had routine tasks of drawing Justin's blood counts by accessing the Mediport and his Central Line. I also administered Justin's chemo treatments, and blood products as needed. Sometimes though, I would just sit with him and talk about anything simply to support him. I will say this. Justin's demeanor was always positive, and was enriched with hope all the time. He was rarely negative and sad, and if he was, you could tell right away that something was really bothering him. When I was with Justin and his family, whether at the clinic or the hospital, it was very difficult to feel like* **just** *a caregiver. I took care of Justin like all of my patients, professionally, but with Justin it was different. To this day I don't know what it was that was different, it just was. I have taken care of many children and their families in my career as a nurse, and some have been very special to me over time. I am sure that will continue in my career, but with Justin and his family, it was just completely different. There always seemed to be something more when it came to Justin. In ways, I guess I never felt that I* **had** *to be strong for the Whitaker family, because I* **always** *felt as a part of their family."*

It was clear that with Kelly, her memories of Justin's final few weeks of life, were deeply painful and rich with emotion. Kelly sullenly said, *"we knew for several weeks that Justin's time was short. I was so grateful that everyone was able to get him to New York City, and most importantly, to Virginia Beach so that he could offer Courtney the 'Promise Ring.' I cannot tell you how important that beach trip was to him, to have the honor of giving Courtney her ring. When he returned from the beach a couple days later, he was admitted into the hospital for the last time. I went to the hospital almost every day, to not only visit with Justin, but with his family and those closest to him as well. Over the course of Justin's illness, I became very close to the entire family, and especially with Barbara and Darrell, his grandparents. I also became very close to Craig toward the end. On the day that the Whitaker's decided to let Justin "go to his true home," I was at the office working. I received a phone call from Dr. Weil telling me to come to the hospital right away. She said that "it was time," and the family requested my presence with them. What an unbelievable showing of love and humility to ask a nurse to be there in the family's most desperate time. I cannot think of a finer compliment to me personally. I spent the entire day there with Justin, his family, Courtney, along with many of Justin's closest friends from school, and throughout the community. There was an amazing outpouring of support and love from so many people. Even after hours passed after his removal from life support, Justin's determination showed through once again, as he valiantly fought, right up to the point of taking a last breath before finally going home."*

Kelly Printz, like everyone else who spoke to me about their admiration for the type of young man Justin was, did not strictly come from her role as a critical care nurse. There was a deepness in their bond that was not common, because Justin was not your typical cancer patient. Far from it. Kelly said, *"to me, Justin had a spirit that was simply overwhelming. He truly made me want to be a better person. He was always so positive and hopeful throughout the majority of his illness. The one and only time I saw sadness within him, was the very last time I saw him alive. He was in our office all day, and I had to give him several blood products, as well as pain medication. When it was about time to leave, as he had done every single time he visited since I first began care for him, he gave me a hug. But, that day's hug was very different. It felt that his hug then, was given to me with so much more love in his heart than usual. It was almost like he knew that he would never see me again. He wanted me to know in his own special way, how much he loved and cared about me. As most people know by now, that was in fact, the very last time I saw Justin alive."*

As Kelly moved on with her thoughts, she also felt the need to relay how Justin always had two distinct sides of him. Kelly noted that, *"Justin just had an amazing, humorous side to him as well, all the while showing me time after time, of his unyielding spirit of love and heart. When I first met Justin with other staff members, he was sixteen years old, and from that moment on, trust me when I say that he spent two full years yearning for the day he was to turn eighteen. Even when he was seventeen, he would come into the clinic and talk of his excitement about turning eighteen soon. I always asked him why, and I already knew the answer, but I knew how much he liked telling me his answer anyway. He would always say that he couldn't wait until he turned eighteen, because he could "then date older women!" He would then give me this look that was difficult to describe, but I know Barbara and Darrell saw it several times, and* **knew** *what that look was all about. That look on his face is one I will never, ever forget. He always had the biggest smile on his face, and it was always enriched with a special glint in his eyes."*

Superman had now passed from this earth, and Kelly felt that the persona taken on by Justin, right up until death, was more than justified. Kelly said, *"the Superman phenomenon took on a life of its own, especially nearing the end of Justin's life. He truly was Superman to so many people. The way that he faced his illness with such determination and hope is a lesson to so many in life, and not just for those facing a terminal illness. Anyone meeting Justin Whitaker learned from this young man. I certainly have. To this day, every time I see anything having to do with Superman, I think of Justin. I think that's EXACTLY what he would like everyone else to do."*

Nearing closure in our discussion, Kelly informed me that she wanted to share something about Justin that she said was *"EXTREMELY personal and special."* Kelly went on to say that she and her husband Warren had been trying to have a baby for almost five years. Kelly said, *"in May of last year, Warren and I were travelling to Connecticut for my brother's college graduation. We were on the I-95 corridor for several hours, and to this day, I don't know what made me do what I did next. I looked over toward the southbound lanes of travel, and I zeroed in on a tractor trailer. On the driver's side door, there was a huge, black Superman shield, with the letters 'J.W.' in neon green. I remember looking to the sky with tears in my eyes saying, o.k. Justin, what are you trying to tell me? Two months after that trip, I became pregnant with twins. After five years of sadness, tears, hope, and determination, I believe that Justin absolutely had something to do with it. After all, he does now have the opportunity to speak to the most powerful being in the world. Over the years when I cared for Justin, he did know about our struggle to have a baby, and Justin always told me "not to worry, and that*

ON THE SEVENTH DAY OF APRIL....SUPERMAN DIED

I would become a mother." Maybe he **did** *have something to do with it after all. I know this as well. On March 11, 2009, when those precious little ones come into this world, I know I will have more than one person watching, praying, and hoping from above."* In a poignant post-script, Kelly and Warren Printz welcomed Madelyn Faith, and Jack Michael into the world on March 11, 2009 at 11:30, and 11:31 a.m. In a lady's way, sweet Madelyn stepped in front of Jack a mere one minute prior. It brought us back to that day way back when, when Kelly Printz sat with Justin Whitaker, as she spoke in frustration of her deep wishes in having a baby. Justin *knew* Kelly's dreams would be realized when he said, *"don't worry Kelly, you will have babies."* Everyone knew by now that Justin's words were *always* true to form.

Of Mentors and Coaches

It was only fitting, that as I sought to speak with North Stafford administrators, teachers, and coaches, that I went first to Justin Whitaker's safe haven...the baseball diamond. It was a hot, mid August day as I drove onto a gravel road accessing the North Stafford baseball field. Head Coach Jim Labrusciano moved toward my truck, and as I walked toward him and shook hands, you sensed right away that he was a leader of young men. Here is baseball season long over, aside from fall ball activities, and Jim was doing what most coaches do in their off time, grooming the diamond. I have been a coach in ice hockey, football, and baseball for the better part of my life, and you can always tell when someone is the *real deal*. Jim *was* that type of guy.

We sat down at an old wooden picnic table near the fence line, and talked about what else...baseball. Justin would have given us that grin and nod to be sure. As we began talking about Justin's death four months prior, you could still clearly see that at times, Jim was pained about the loss. We spoke about his brief words at Justin's memorial service, and I commented that it must have been very hard for him. Jim said, *"I have a nerve problem in my right arm, and the kids all knew that at times, I would get sore from throwing endless sessions of batting practice. That is why at the service I mentioned of sometimes being in pain, yet all I have to do at those times is imagine the pain Justin went through on a regular basis, and my pains were nothing in comparison."*

The subject of *Superman* came up, and like most, Coach Labrusciano talked about the amazing effect it seemed to have on so many people. Jim said, *"when he took on that Superman persona in the hospital, he took it to heart, and in very special ways, it offered hope to the many young children that Justin spent time with in the ICU. Justin took their illnesses on his shoulders, and even if he was personally in pain, you would never know it from his demeanor. I think in many ways it was a coping mechanism for Justin's father Craig, all the family members, and*

ON THE SEVENTH DAY OF APRIL...SUPERMAN DIED

Courtney too. It served as a rallying cry of sorts, and it helped ease her mind and heart as Justin's role of Superman came into play."

Jim reflected back on the first time he saw Justin play at North Stafford during his sophomore year. He watched as Justin truly battled for the left fielder's position, and how tenacious and full of energy he was. Jim also remembered how hard Justin was on himself at times. *"There were times that if he either struck out or made any out for that matter, that he would trot back toward the dugout with his shoulders and head pointing downwards. There were times he would apologize to me for making an out. I would try to encourage him and he would dig in and try even harder the next time. That first fall when I saw him, he really contributed a lot to the team. He then hurt his knee, and then it seemed a very short time later, he was diagnosed with his illness. He never gave up though. I'll give him that. Never!"*

Jim seemed to pause momentarily, lost in thought, and said *"you know, I just remembered this and had almost forgotten it. There was one time when Justin and I were watching the Oklahoma and Miami football game. Justin was having a great time as we talked about our favorite teams, and thinking about it now, really makes me treasure that moment. I say that because when Justin started to get sick and was weakening, that same vibrant personality kicked in. In many ways, I think that is how he coped, and was always able to deflect questions about his own physical pains, and what he was going through. I truly believed that this was his way of easing his deepest senses of anguish. As we watched the game, Justin told me that his favorite college football team was Michigan. Contact was later made with Michigan Head Football Coach, Rich Rodriguez, who later called Justin and sent him a lot of Wolverine souvenirs. Justin was so touched by that gesture. I was always amazed at the way a boy his age fought his illness. He was a warrior."*

Coach Labrusciano talked about how all of Stafford County seemingly bonded together as Justin battled his cancer. He was equally overwhelmed by the way opposing teams rallied around Justin and his family as well. Jim said, *"as I watched kids from all over at the candlelight vigil after Justin passed away, you could clearly see that the bitterness you would normally see from rival school members at times, was simply not present. Everyone there was grieving over one of their peers. I really think most of the kids grew up quickly when they first realized how sick Justin was, and then how an eighteen year old can be taken from this life. I have great pride in saying that the North Stafford administrators,* teachers, coaches, and student body handled things incredibly well from start to finish. The manner in which our administration prepared an entire school for Justin's impending death, seemed to truly galvanize everyone together."

Courtney's parents, Steve and Val, echoed similar praises as Coach Labrusciano. Val remarked, *"NSHS and Stafford County is, and will always be tops in our hearts. Everyone truly stepped up to the plate for Justin and his family. I think as we watched the swell of support for Justin, it helped us deal with the ever changing situations with all of his medical issues. I think it gave Justin's family strength as well, knowing that he was being helped and supported in ways that cannot be understood or imagined. The entire staff and the coaches at NSHS were amazing. They gave Courtney opportunities to put her thoughts, emotions, struggles, and hopes together and make it manageable, so that she could always remain positive for Justin. You have to understand that every waning moment, Court was always wondering "how I can help Justin more," or "am I doing enough?" NSHS and the wonderful citizens of Stafford County and beyond, gave Justin hope simply by opening the doors to their hearts, and doing everything they could to help. We could not even believe the overwhelming love and support every step of the way. It just proves to all of us how letting your heart lead the way at times like this makes this journey in life amazing. Our family carries both great emotion, and difficulty trying to explain how much everyone's sincere care and love for Justin touched our hearts. What really stood out for us, was the ways in which the NSHS 2008 Senior Class surrounded Justin's family and ours with such love, courage, and strength. It was unbelievable! Without the support of Courtney's friends that helped her through such difficult times, along with her mentor and trainer, Dave Gonier, I honestly don't think she could have pulled through it in the ways that she did. We will forever be indebted to everyone during this dreadful crisis."*

With four months passed since Justin's death, I could tell that at certain times during our discussions, this rough and tumble coach was still grieving over the loss of his young, student athlete. When asked how he handled addressing his team as a group, when news was passed on that Justin's condition was worsening, Jim put his head down slightly, and sadly said, *"I told the boys that they all had to prepare for the worst. I spoke to them as more of a father figure because we were a close knit team, and I knew that they were all hurting in one way or another. I talked to them about supporting each other, and about stepping up as Justin would expect. I was amazed at how the seniors*

ON THE SEVENTH DAY OF APRIL....SUPERMAN DIED

stepped up to the plate. Nate Moore, Casey Johns, and John Tate all seemed to rally the troops and take the younger players under their wings. Our ace pitcher Zack Miller came up to me after and said, "this really wakes you up coach. I'm eighteen years old and have always thought that nothing can happen to me, and now I am losing one of my best friends." I am proud of my team and everyone who supported them this past season. I don't think anything was as hard as this situation."

As Jim and I talked on, it was inevitable that we began speaking about how Courtney and Justin's family handled all of this with such strength, and courage. Jim said, *"I tell you what. I know that I would not have been able to handle things in the ways that they did. I have young children, and was hurting very badly. I had a lot of sleepless nights. I was called at night and informed of Justin's death, and I handled tons of calls with kids until about 3:30 a.m. As a father, Craig amazed me. I would think to myself that if this was my boy, I would have flipped out by now, but his strength, and courage was absolutely amazing. For Courtney to maintain her grades, train for softball, and spend countless hours at the hospital day in and day out, is a testament to that same sense of immense strength and courage. I am not sure if I would have been so strong."*

Coach Labrusciano spoke numerous times about the community rallying around Justin, and said he was inundated by calls from coaches from all over Virginia, Maryland, and into D.C. Everyone had been following Justin's story for the past two years, and they all voiced compassion and care. Jim was emotionally touched by many calls he received from parents throughout Stafford County, who also had children afflicted with some type of cancer. In ways similar to how Justin had handled his illness, the parents seemed to share a common, inspirational theme. They learned to fight terrible illness because of Justin Whitaker. Jim added, *"cancer touches everyone, and I think that with someone like Justin, anything positive that people can latch onto, and manage to spin something positive out of it is worthwhile. I believe that those I spoke to about Justin's illness, did just that."*

As we were finishing our conversation, members of the Wolverine's fall baseball team began to arrive. I asked Jim if anything came to mind now about Justin's passing, that he had not really thought of before. He took a deep breath and told me that *"I am always around all the boys, and it was so very hard to stay composed all the time. I still wear his wristband every day, and I have Justin and Courtney's senior picture in my house that I always glance at. I was just thinking about something the other day. My five year old son continues to ask me when he will be able to see Justin again? He says, "daddy will I see him soon?" It breaks my heart to hear that question, and know that he doesn't completely grasp Justin's death. One day the two of us were getting our hair cut, and the barber was talking to my son, and I heard Justin's name being mentioned. At first I was a little taken aback by the conversation, until I heard the barber say, "I know the whole Whitaker family. I knew Justin too, and cut his hair, Jordie's, and their dad's." All of a sudden I felt this happiness come over me because here we were on the far end of Spotsylvania County, and someone else was remembering Justin and keeping his spirit alive."*

Before I got into my truck I asked if anything would be done at the baseball field to honor Justin. Jim said the plans were to hopefully install a new scoreboard, and to have Justin's name on the base of it. Along with that, a memorial stone was to be engraved and placed somewhere to the rear of the home plate area. I later had the chance to see this memorial stone in the front office of North Stafford High School. It was fittingly shaped like home plate. At the top, it had Justin's name, with his cherished number seven below. At the base were the words, *'Gone But Not Forgotten,'* with the last notation of 'Class of 2008.' In the future, anyone who took the field in Wolverine country, would forever be reminded of number seven, and his days playing baseball there. His father Craig poignantly reminded us so long ago, *"his legacy will never be forgotten."* That is without debate.

As the dog days of August moved in, the North Stafford football team was digging in for another season. One of the Wolverine football coaches, Don Casias, had previously coached in baseball, and was very close to Justin since middle school. Don remembered the tall skinny kid from Rodney Thompson Middle School in Stafford, Virginia. He laughed for a second and recalled Justin with a tight, crew cut hairstyle. Even way back when in middle school, Justin was all about baseball. Justin knew that Don used to work within the Cincinnati Reds organization, which further stoked Justin's baseball fires.

ON THE SEVENTH DAY OF APRIL....SUPERMAN DIED

As middle school ended, Don knew that Justin went to Colonial Forge, but after one semester, Justin transferred to Wolverine land. Don said, *"Justin was always a great kid. I remember him his freshman year. He was all about baseball, and always full of energy when he talked to you."* During his sophomore year, Coach Casias said that Justin suffered a knee injury, and became very depressed that it was not going to heal in time for the start of baseball. Don added that, *"I had a sports medicine and strength/conditioning background, so I worked with Justin as far as getting better and stronger once his knee injury healed. The thing that I remember most about Justin, was how he took my son Michael, who was twelve at the time, and worked with him. Justin never had to do that, but I watched as he played soft toss with him, and helped him adjust his batting swing. Justin basically mentored my son when his knee was not 100%, and I will never forget his generosity, and the ways in which he showed Michael things on the side. I could tell by his instruction, that one day, Justin would have made one incredible coach. He just had that way about him."*

As Justin began getting better, Don said that, *"Coach Labrusciano and I talked about using him in a designated hitter's role. We knew he was a solid hitter, but that he would still have limitations running. Another thing that struck me whenever I was around Justin, was the sheer fact that he was so fiery, and competitive. He wanted to play so badly, he would do anything humanly possible to get out there on that baseball field. As coaches, you see some athletes barely trying sometimes, or they go halfway. That was never the case with Justin."* Don remembered Justin dating Courtney at the time too, and always saw them together everywhere.

Just as it seemed that Justin was rounding the corner with his knee and getting more comfortable each day, the coaching staff was told about Justin's diagnosis of cancer. Don said *"Jim (Coach Labrusciano) called to say that Justin was diagnosed with cancer, and that they had to rush him to the hospital. It hit me like a ton of bricks. I just had a co-worker go through cancer with her two twins, and was devastated over that. We both knew Justin well, so it hit her hard too. Luckily today, both of the kids are in remission, but I will never forget all of the things that went through my mind. Jim and I got to the hospital, and what blew me away was the fact that Justin immediately apologized for his illness, almost in a way that said he had let the team down with his cancer. Justin looked at us both and said, 'I'm so sorry. I'm going to beat this coach." To say I was stunned was an understatement. As more and more people arrived to see Justin at the hospital, I remember how he always portrayed that strong front. Courtney did too. They never let you see or feel what was going on behind the scenes. That always amazed me."*

Don went on to talk more about Justin's cancer and said, *"here he is just clearing things up, and getting a green light after his knee injury, and now this?"* Don said it seemed at times like a roller coaster ride. The lumps that had been enlarged in Justin's neck started to go down, and it appeared his white cell count was getting down to where they should be. Don said that *"when the chemotherapy ended, somehow we all believed that because of Justin's spirit and fight, that he was going to beat this. There were so many in his family, and so many kids supporting him at every turn, that things were really looking up. It was so sad to see things move into a remission state, and then have the cancer return with such force."*

Justin's junior year saw cancer spreading again. Don was stunned in seeing Courtney remaining so calm, and composed the entire time. Don said, *"she had all her school work, athletics, and everything else going on but she never let Justin feel alone, or think that he was fighting this by himself."* Around the time of the bone marrow transplant failure, Don said that there was an overwhelming feeling that Justin may be on a final turn. Don went on to say, *"I was always upfront and honest with Justin and all my athletes. One day I said, tell me how you are feeling Justin? He said that his feet were really swollen and very sore, and his legs, and arms were very tender."* It was at this point when Coach Casias began to painfully drift back to that moment, as he became emotionally upset. With tears welling in his eyes, Don went on to add that, *"one time when I walked into his room, he had terrible sores on his mouth. We were all alone and I said to Justin, let's talk about anything you want. It doesn't have to be about your cancer. You name it and we can talk about it. I looked at him in that bed and asked him, Justin, tell me what we can do for you? Justin for the very first time with me, broke down crying."* Once again Coach Casias, when talking to me, struck another one of his hidden, internal nerves. His eyes welled up in tears as he told me that as Justin cried, all he said was, *"coach, I am so worried about my brother, my dad, my mother...Courtney."* I could not believe that he was lying in that bed with his life on the line, but he spoke of how much he worried about his own family first.

ON THE SEVENTH DAY OF APRIL...SUPERMAN DIED

Don and I talked about Justin and Courtney's last trip, when he was going to give her the promise ring. Don sadly said, *"I think before Justin left for Virginia Beach, he knew that he was going to die soon. It was so like Justin. He had a very special thing to do with Courtney, and all the while in his mind, I think he really knew that he would not be around much longer. Courtney later showed me the ring, and the saddest part of it all was when I asked her how Justin was doing. She said he was sick again, and in my heart, I had a feeling that the end was near. It was very devastating for me. I teach an anatomy and physiology class, and I knew that we would be talking about cancer. Everyone was aware of Justin's situation, but each time I hit that topic, it was very, very painful for me. About one month after Justin's death, the mother of one of our other players, Robert Kohn, died of cancer as well. The North Stafford family again, took it very hard."*

Knowing that Coach Casias was hurrying to get ready for a football scrimmage, we changed directions once again, and talked about the other teams from the Commonwealth District. Don said, *"whenever I walked into the gym for the memorial service, and saw the whole District represented by all the players and coaches honoring Justin, it was absolutely amazing. There was no bitterness, or talk of rivals. For the rest of the season, all the baseball teams honored Justin with warm up shirts bearing his initials and number seven, and none of them had to do that. It was a fine thing to do by everyone all the way around."*

I knew that I couldn't let Coach Casias walk away without commenting on the phenomenon associated with *Superman Whitaker*. As soon as I brought it up, Don laughed, and remembered one time when he went to visit Justin and said, *"so you are Superman huh...a man of steel? Justin jokingly pointed to all the bruises on both arms, and to all the wires and tubes attached to his body. He even made mention of pain killers coursing through his body, but he made light of it and never complained. I was thinking to myself, how is that even possible? We had a few laughs over the whole Superman thing, but there was no doubt in my mind. He was that character for sure."* Don said that he got the chance to watch Justin interact with younger cancer patients on the ward, and said that *"Justin was absolutely loved. The nurses loved him, and the kids adored how he treated them, even when he was in so much pain all the time. I think personally, that Justin brought great attention to what cancer really is, and the effects it has on everyone involved. He faced his cancer head on, and I think because of that, he gave cancer a face, and made everyone aware of its meaning."*

As we neared closure talking about Justin's life, and his connection to Coach Casias, I asked him if there was some things that were personal to him, that he had not really shared with anyone before. Don paused for a minute, and his eyes welled with tears again. He said, *"I see my son Michael, and in him, I see so many similarities with Justin. My son Michael knew Justin a little better than most of the sophomores that year, and he was only a freshman. I know he spoke with my wife about Justin's death, and has not really said much since, but I know he took Justin's death very hard."*

Don said he still worries about the entire Whitaker family, Courtney, Zac, and everyone touched by Justin. Don said, *"everyone will need their own time and place to get over the fact that Justin has passed. I told Zac and a lot of our guys, that Justin's death, in a way, can be seen as a gift. I talked about how he had impacted everyone's life, and because of that, ten, or twenty years from now at reunions, everyone will always remember Justin for what he meant to them during his life. He left on his own terms. He didn't want to go, but he absolutely left on his own terms. He had two years to prepare for the worst and never gave up. That should be a lesson to everyone."* Don began tearing up again as we finished up and left me with this. *"Justin Whitaker showed all of us, and especially me as a father, how valuable your children really are. You learn from all of this, and you remain thankful for each day you have with them. Your kids can be taken from you at the snap of fingers, and Justin showed us all how to live, and when facing the end, he taught us again how fragile life is."*

Late August finds teachers and coaches prepping to return to classrooms, and hot, steamy playing fields. I met with the North Stafford junior varsity field hockey coach, Leigh Swift, along with fellow teacher, Nicole Hagermann. Nicole had coached cross country for the last four years as well. Courtney and the Whitaker family had told me how close Justin had become with them toward the end of his life. Leigh served as the Student Class Association Sponsor, and was proud to explain that through all of the fundraising efforts accomplished through North Stafford High School, they were able to raise close to $25,000 toward defraying costs for Justin's medical expenses. Leigh and Nicole in unison though, said that the support for Justin moved far beyond raising money.

ON THE SEVENTH DAY OF APRIL....SUPERMAN DIED

Leigh explained to me that she had Courtney in her classes for all four years, but it was only when Justin became ill in his junior year, that she came to know who he truly was as a person. Following Justin's diagnosis, Leigh worked with Courtney, Nicole, and others in trying to come up with ideas to raise funds. Nicole had been at North Stafford for five years, and served as the Senior Class Sponsor.

Leigh was always stunned whenever she spoke with Justin, as he constantly thanked her for all of the work accomplished on his behalf. Leigh added, *"he would never complain about what he was going through, and our conversations always ended with a thank you and a big hug. That was Justin. I would see Courtney every day too, day in and day out, and she worked hard all the time to get everything done."* Nicole said that she got to know Justin this past year, and said that, *"when everyone was at the school cooking on that Friday, which was the night before we were going to have the dinner and talent show for Justin, we were all in the kitchen working until about nine o'clock that night. Justin was going to take Courtney to a sports game that night, but before he left to go, he stopped in the kitchen and hugged every single person in the room. He thanked everyone for all their help and then left with Courtney. I knew then what kind of a person he was."*

As it related to the show Nicole spoke of on February 2, 2008, Courtney and Zac had a fitting tribute with a play on the letters of 'Superman.' Before they introduced the beginning talent acts, they performed a hip hop ditty and took turns, spelling the 'Superman' name with a word that they picked for each that described who Justin was. The words chosen with the letters were; S—*Strength*, U—*Unique*, P—*Perseverance*, E—*Extraordinary*, R—*Rambo*, M—*Man*, A—*Admirable*, and N—*Nemesis*. Justin and his baseball mates surprised those in the audience by removing their suit jackets and shirts, revealing Superman emblazoned shirts underneath. Craig Whitaker said later, *"we were all shocked but to our family, the Superman theme for this incredible night was now complete."*

As I sat and talked about Justin, you could feel the manner in which Leigh and Nicole felt for him, even if their times conversing, or getting to know all of the details of his life were limited. The one common theme that arose again and again, regardless of who you spoke to, was Justin's demeanor as he faced his illness. Similar to what Leigh had said, Nicole remarked that *"Justin would always have a nice smile on his face. You would never know that anything bad was ever going on, and when he left you, it was always with a hug. He was always positive all the time and very thankful for everything. If there was something bad happening, Courtney would fill us in, but Justin just remained consistently steady."*

It almost seemed surreal that over four months had passed since Justin's death, yet as we talked about him, there was little doubt within the eyes of Leigh and Nicole, as to the effects Justin had on their lives. Leigh softly remarked that she *"was blessed that I was a small part of Justin's world. Courtney, and then the entire Whitaker family, basically invited me into their lives. The community surrounding Justin and his family was absolutely overwhelming."* Leigh and Nicole spoke about the dinner and show planned to raise money for Justin, and were actually worried that they may not sell the four hundred tickets for the event. Both were shocked at how many people showed up, and the incredible generosity displayed. Nicole said, *"we sold every ticket, and there were virtually no seats left. It was a standing room only crowd, and as we glanced at the food disappearing, we had to order pizzas to make sure everyone had something to eat. The teachers and all the employees at North Stafford were so unselfish as well, not only because of their busy schedules and duties, but strictly because they had very little time to themselves. It never mattered. Whenever anyone mentioned anything about something that had to be done for Justin, everyone seemed to stop what they were doing and chipped in. Even before and after Justin's memorial service, people who never even knew Justin would either donate money to the fund, or help out in any way they could behind the scenes. There was this amazing family feel to it all."*

Both Leigh and Nicole commented on how all of the Commonwealth District schools, especially the sports teams, set rivalries aside and honored Justin as one of their own. Leigh added, *"the area schools had their own fund raising efforts for Justin, and everyone unified and pulled together. I remember after the dinner and show how all the seniors, dressed in black and white, signed a huge photo mat for Justin, making it a perfect evening for him. Everything done for him was from the heart and so touching. Even as we were all mourning, as a group we all seemed to step back and say to each other, what do we have to do next? This is what a family does."* Leigh added, *"from my last visit with Justin, to the candlelight vigil, you could feel the pain as everyone grieved, but then we shifted gears* because there was so much to do for the Whitaker family. Nicole and I had to support a lot of people, cover classes, and plan with the whole school for Justin's memorial service. I can't say enough about the administrators, and staff at North Stafford as they helped Nicole and I at every turn. We were all family."

When I began discussing the mourning processes that come with every death, once again, I could see that Leigh and Nicole held some private thoughts within. Nicole said that even with time passing by after Justin's death, she will *"always see and feel him as an angel."* Leigh nodded her head in firm concurrence. Leigh said, *"Justin's death made me really think about the smaller things in life that we all worry about every day. Now it is not that big of a deal compared to what he went through. Justin had huge issues in his fight, and he faced them all, setting an example for all of us."* As we neared the end of our talk, Nicole commented about Craig Whitaker, marveling at his strength every step of the way. *"To me, Craig served as an inspirational model for me to follow. I found myself in awe as he and Courtney remained so focused on what was hurting everyone else, and they worried more about their feelings. Craig literally opened the door to everything in the family, good or bad, and his strength was incredible."* As we prepared to say goodbye, I asked Leigh and Nicole if there was any one thing they could say that spoke of the sad tragedy of Justin's passing. Leigh said, *"Nicole and I talked about all that we went through individually. It was definitely the highlight of our professional careers. We did all we could do, and honored Justin in life, and then in death, in the best ways we knew how. It was a true honor for us to do anything we could to help."*

My next visit to North Stafford High School, lead me into the Guidance Office, and a talk with Justin's primary Guidance Counselor, Diana Smithey. I was not quite sure what I was feeling during the drive down Rt. 610 to the school, but I found myself recalling Diana speaking at Justin's memorial service, and the poignant words she used when interviewed by regional news reporters. Somehow, I had a feeling that once we began speaking to one another in her office, that it was going to be deeply moving and emotional. I could not put a finger on it, but I just knew.

I met Diana in the outer office and walked to her small room a few feet away. We sat down and began talking about the first occasion when she met Justin Whitaker. Ms. Smithey believed that it was sometime in the latter stages of Justin's freshman year. We were both aware that Justin had transferred from Colonial Forge, but it was unclear as to the exact time he arrived at North Stafford. Nonetheless, Diana said that she recalled speaking to Justin as a result of a group of people he was with. As many people have remarked about before, she vividly remembered how Justin had that wry smile on his face, a mischievous expression, but a smile that she will never forget. From that moment on, it was the smile of Justin Whitaker that has always stayed with her.

At the end of Justin's sophomore year, Diana was shocked to learn that he had been diagnosed with cancer. Diana recalled that, *"at the time, Justin was recovering from a knee injury and was on crutches. I conferred with Coach Labrusciano to see if he had heard the terrible news of Justin's diagnosis, and my heart sunk when he confirmed it. I remember how in the school, maybe because Justin was so young and competitive, that we talked amongst ourselves, hoping that it may be a minor lymph node problem. My first reaction to the diagnosis was astonishment, because I knew nothing about his illness."* It was at this juncture in time, that the issue of Justin possibly being readied for the 'Homebound Instruction' program, may be necessary.

Diana spoke softly at times, as she reflected on her conversations with Justin on topics far removed from strictly that of cancer. Diana said, *"I don't think I can ever recall Justin speaking negatively about his illness, and what may happen as time moved on. Even at the point when his bone marrow transplant failed, when most would falter, Justin seemingly fought on. I could see pain in his eyes though, but no matter what, he always found a way for you to see his smile too. There was one time when I asked him flat out if he was in pain. Justin would only say, "I'll be alright Mrs. Smithey. Don't worry about me."* As Diana said those words, it was amazing to me how many people I spoke to, echoed those same phrases. Here was a young man fighting for his life, yet he sought no favors or shortcuts, and forever cared more for you than he wanted you to *ever* worry about him.

When asked if Justin ever showed any signs of emotional distress, Diana remarked that, *"there was one time when I went to visit Justin in the hospital. He started to talk to me as tears welled up in his eyes and he said, "I miss school so much Mrs. Smithey." As he spoke I felt his pain, and his father Craig also began to cry because there was so much emotion behind his simple words."*

ON THE SEVENTH DAY OF APRIL....SUPERMAN DIED

The entire time while sitting with Diana, I felt the immense respect she had for Justin. It was not simply because that was her duty, or her compassion for a young person suffering from a dreadful illness. She respected Justin Whitaker as the *man* he was facing everything head on. Diana went on to say, *"his dignity was so much a part of his character, as if to say, even if I spend a little time with someone, I want it to be a good time. It was amazing to me that Justin stayed so strong, and his presence could be felt by anyone in the same room with him. He was forever hopeful, and he would speak to me without ever complaining or saying why me?"* I will admit that I was absolutely floored when Diana referred to something Justin had said. One day when the subject of "why me" came up, Justin told Diana, *"if I say why me, then I am wishing it on someone else. If someone has to have cancer, then let it be me. I would not wish it on anyone else but me. Let it be me."* At that moment, in Diana Smithey's cramped office, I found myself tearing up, and once again, I felt that painful lump arise in my throat again. This was not a little boy dealing with cancer, and aimlessly wondering about its consequences. This was a young man who was forced to quickly grow up, and accept the darkest of the dark, and do so without wincing. Justin Whitaker would never wish away his unfortunate illness on another innocent person. It was just not his style.

Ms. Smithey and I talked in general terms about all of the children she works with, and of her role as a teacher of young people. Diana turned and said, *"my relationship with Justin offered me lesson after lesson learned. I was not in a position to teach him anything, and I am sure that he never knew how many things he was teaching me along the way. There was one time when I talked quietly with Justin and he said, "do I want all of this to be over Mrs. Smithey? Absolutely! But, I would be a fool to believe I can wish it all away." That was Justin Whitaker."*

As Justin's illness progressed and seemingly worsened, I asked Diana if she ever truly knew of all of the procedures going on, or if she could ever tell when, or if something was going bad with Justin's health. Diana said, *"most of the time as I learned of medical procedures to be done for Justin, I would either find out through Craig or Courtney. But, for fear of others inaccurately forwarding this information through the school or beyond, it was kept very quiet and within a small, family circle. To watch Craig and Courtney deal with things along the way was amazing. I believe they fed off of each other's strengths. To watch as*

Courtney completed all her school work, trained in athletics, stood by Justin's side at every turn, and tried to maintain her own personal life, was nothing short of miraculous."

The subject of one's purpose in life came up and for a few seconds, Diana was quiet and did not speak right away. As she did, it was almost as if she was conjuring up images of Justin, recapturing his persona as she said, *"within his short life, he fulfilled a purpose, while offering so many messages. Some of us may live an entire life and never know what purposes are served along the way. For me, Justin served as a teacher of sorts. He showed me how to live with dignity. In him I could clearly see the perfect image of courage in totality. Through Justin, I learned of the good that arises in life, from someone with absolutely nothing good happening to him. Even in his silence, Justin Whitaker served as a teacher for me. His demeanor never changed, nor did that smile. Honestly, when Justin smiled, you could never differentiate it from the healthy Justin, to the one who was so very sick."*

When we talked about Justin's 'Homebound Instruction' work at North Stafford, Diana perked up right away, and wanted me to know right off the bat that Justin had gone above and beyond the call of duty. Diana remembered someone once asking if Justin was given free credits toward the end of the program to satisfy the graduation remarks. She was adamant in explaining that regarding *all* of Justin's assignments, he stayed on top of things in every regard. He would constantly say to Diana, *"Mrs. Smithey, is there anything else that I need to do to make sure that I am doing the same work as everyone in the classes?"* Diana commented on this further, saying *"Justin was so dignified as an individual and student, that he would never accept less work than that which was assigned to every other student who attended class on a daily basis. He read every book, and did every assignment to complete satisfaction of all his 'Homebound Instruction' teachers."*

Diana told me that it was vitally important to Justin, that he earned the required credits for his high school diploma before his bone marrow transplant procedure. Diana recalled that *"Justin would constantly call me, and ask repeatedly if all his school work was tabulated, and that he was remaining on track to graduate. Even when I assured him that he was perfectly aligned with all that he needed to accomplish, he would again ask me over and over if I was absolutely sure that he was lined up to graduate."*

ON THE SEVENTH DAY OF APRIL....SUPERMAN DIED

As news of Justin's failed bone marrow transplant started spreading through North Stafford, Diana Smithey distinctly remembered that there was a pall cast throughout every area of the school. Diana said, *"it was at that point in time when I think that if people were denying his illness, they were all hit hard by the reality that he may not survive much longer. Once again, it was Courtney who shared all the grim facts of Justin's condition, and between Courtney and Craig, I honestly don't know how they made it through each day. To think of Courtney as an eighteen year old woman was not possible, because her maturity was far above most. She shared the saddest pieces of information detailing Justin's medical condition with great strength and courage. It was never done out of weakness, just sheer strength. You always knew that what she was saying was honest and accurate, but equally distressing. The remarkable thing about Justin was, right after his transplant was done, he called me at school and wanted to make sure that he could start up with his final stages of 'Homebound Instruction.' That spoke volumes for the type of person Justin Whitaker was, as both a caring, loving human being, and a focused, diligent student."*

Ms. Smithey was truly amazed at how the entire county rallied around Justin, to the point where total strangers who had never crossed his path, would ask "what can I do to help?" Diana remarked, *"I talked to so many people who told me how much they had been affected by Justin's situation, and how that alone served as the impetus for changing something in their lives. The community came together for a common cause, and Justin Whitaker was the reason for such heartfelt love and support. I remember one person, Justin's former baseball coach Craig Lopez. Craig had taken over head coaching duties at Mountain View High School when they opened. He called to ask if* **"we** *(the entire Mountain View family) could do anything to help Justin out?" The calls never stopped, and the people never stopped coming into North Stafford to ask what they could do?"*

Following the dinner and talent show in February of 2008, at Justin's request, only those in his family, and those he was closest to, remained behind at North Stafford High School so that he could receive his diploma in a private ceremony. It was not that Justin wanted to exclude all of the North Stafford students from watching him receive his diploma, but it was a private, special time to spend with his loved ones. North Stafford school personnel were present, and donned graduation caps and gowns with Justin. Diana said with immense pride, *"to see that look in his* eyes as he received his diploma was priceless. He earned that diploma under the most trying of times, and those who loved him were there by his side. That picture you see of Justin smiling with his diploma in hand is something I will never forget. I turned to face Justin during the ceremony, and mouthed the words, "you did it," and he was absolutely beaming. It was incredibly emotional."

Diana Smithey made numerous comments to me that were echoed by virtually everyone who spoke to me about Justin Whitaker. She looked at me at times with saddened eyes, and a mournful expression, yet she also talked with great conviction and strength about a person she admired in life. One of the things Diana said that was very deserving, entailed Justin's *Superman* nickname. Diana said, "*maybe it was Justin's youthful age, and how he courageously battled his illness at every turn. People around him grasped the Superman name because it now had Justin Whitaker's name attached to it. People could easily identify Justin as a super hero because he never blinked when fighting a horrible enemy. I think being labeled as Superman allowed outsiders as well, to align with the countless stories of bravery and battles that Justin endured for over two years. Was Justin Superman? There is no doubt in my mind that he was.*"

Diana talked briefly to me about her family, and specifically her son who had graduated from North Stafford High School in 2003. Diana softly said, "*my son never personally knew Justin Whitaker, but he understood my role as a counselor who had a great deal of contact with him. My son, who never knew this person, asked about Justin and of his courage in dealing with cancer. There were so many times when it was so emotional for me. But, the last thing I wanted to do was to cry in front of others, and take away any positive feelings that family members, and close friends had, regardless of how bad everything was. My son was a person of great support for me. He told me that I could let it all out and cry, and believe me, there were times when I was so down and struggled so much. I guess on those days, I chose not to call and hear Justin's voice. It would have been too much to bear at certain points, so I always tried to exhibit a strong front.*"

As we were nearing an end to our conversation that bordered two hours (actually feeling more like fifteen minutes), Diana and I talked about her inner most private moments and times dealing with Justin's illness. Diana took a long pause, and again, I can only guess that she was reflecting on past days spent with Justin as she said, "*I had my private moments, trust me. As parents, it is so difficult to see another person's child in pain, especially when there is very little you can do about it. There was one private conversation I had with Justin. I said one day while visiting him, Justin, if you ever want to talk to me about anything, you can tell me anything. I wish there was a magic wand that I could wave to make this all better for you. All Justin said in response was, "I'm o.k. Mrs. Smithey. I'm alright. But, if I'm not, I will let you know." When he said that, I was stunned at his maturity amidst such dire circumstances. Here was a young man facing death, yet he wanted me to know he was o.k...simply amazing."*

As we discussed the Whitaker family in general, Diana was very pointed in saying that, *"with Justin and Jordie as children, I gave Craig great credit in how they were as people...caring, loving, respectful, and kind. I felt that whatever it was that gave the boys such warmth and character, was either in their blood, or instilled by Craig, and other loving family members. There is something so inherently special about the entire Whitaker family, and I include the grandparents as well. There is a sweetness, and kindness that to me, remains indescribable. Their demeanor in the most trying of times, always entailed sentiments of hope and optimism, that somehow had a way to overshadow their immense sadness. I am not the same person now as I was then, because of all that I felt from Justin's inner circle of loved ones."*

In our final few minutes of conversation, I asked Diana how Justin's illness, and ultimately his death, had changed or altered her life. Once again, I felt Diana Smithey's heart and soul arise as she took a few minutes to gather her thoughts. After a few moments, Diana said, *"Justin's passing has changed my whole view about my life, and especially my job here at North Stafford as a guidance counselor, seeking to make a difference in the lives of students. Shortly after Justin's death, I asked myself that maybe I was not here to make a difference, but rather to feel the differences that others around me may be experiencing. I find now that I want to learn from other students as well. I realize that I am in a position within the school to influence students. But, through all of my time spent with Justin, I came away knowing today how much I can learn from so many other young people. Justin Whitaker had immense, internal power. It was the kind of personal power I have seen and felt from great leaders. He never, ever preached to people. He was simply a powerful, powerful soul who moved people in every imaginable way. His power had ways to grip everyone around him who he touched. It never mattered who you were, to Justin you were a friend. To me, Justin*

Whitaker fulfilled a special purpose. The beauty of that purpose is that it was so fulfilling and different from one person to the next. Justin was a person just fighting to live as a teenager, and enjoy life every step of the way. To me, his purpose...his message, gave hope to us all without Justin ever having to say a word. That to me was the man I came to admire...Justin Whitaker."

I was personally so touched and moved by all of Diana Smithey's words, that I walked out of her office and climbed into my truck, feeling emotionally drained in similar fashion to how I felt following Justin's death. Her words were beyond poignant, and her heart and soul seemed to speak for everyone who ever met Justin. You felt every word, and through all of her loving, sincere comments, I was able to bring visions of Justin back to me. Diana remarked numerous times about Justin's smile, and how it seemingly lit up a room. It did far more than that.

It was now the end of September 2008, and North Stafford was in full swing as students had returned with classes, and sports beginning anew. I sat down with Principal Thomas Nichols, and the Wolverine's Athletic Director, Margaret Lowry. Tom and Margaret were to be my final interviews at the school, and as we sat down, I could sense that long before they spoke, that our talk about Justin would be very special. Margaret talked of meeting Justin for the first time, and remembered that he had just transferred from cross town rival, Colonial Forge. She recalled Justin having his knee injury back then, and of his optimism at fighting back hard so he could get back on the baseball field. Tom remarked, *"it's funny, but I remember seeing Justin and Zac walking through the front doors, always joking, and smiling. Justin always seemed to be carrying his baseball bat. Then I remember the shock setting in with everyone here, when after his knee injury, he was diagnosed with cancer. But even then, you could never see it in Justin. His optimism, and drive always made you believe he would beat his illness."* Margaret added that, *"I still see Justin now, even after he was diagnosed, trying to bounce back and get back on that ball field. Just by seeing him push on, it gave everyone hope that he would beat his sickness. He had to leave school quite a bit in the early stages as he underwent treatments, and he did get back on that field. He never quite re-captured a starting position, but I was in awe at how hard he worked."*

ON THE SEVENTH DAY OF APRIL....SUPERMAN DIED

Both Tom Nichols and Margaret Lowry watched on the periphery, as the Whitaker family, Courtney, Zac, and countless others did all they could to lessen the endless burdens. Margaret said, *"from constant fund raising efforts, to watching Justin's father Craig, and his family juggle busy work schedules, and their lives in general, there was never any quit in anyone. If you watched Justin push on and on, and see everyone around him sharing that same optimistic attitude, you would never have thought his illness would ever have terminal consequences."* Tom went on to say that Courtney was often the main source of information, as it related to Justin's condition. Tom remembered that *"one day Courtney was very excited and upbeat, saying that Justin was beating his illness, and was so thrilled that he was in remission. Good news would then begin to flow throughout the whole school, and then suddenly, we would be stung by bad news. It had that up and down feel to it for so much of the time."*

One thing that both Margaret and Thomas did agree on, was the ground swell of support that grew to amazing levels, especially toward the end as Justin's condition waned. Tom said that *"you would have younger students, or just those that never personally knew Justin, but you would never know it by how everyone rallied around him and his family. During Justin's junior year when he returned to school, so many kids had on their 'Welcome Back Superman' shirts, which to me, was so important in so many ways. I think that is why the memorial service was so touching. Justin's fight brought out so much optimism and passion in everyone, that it turned into this massive state of community bonding that I had never seen before. There is no doubt in my mind that Justin was that superhero, because it absolutely fit. No matter how many pieces of bad news Justin received, or how sick he was, he was an anchor of optimism."* Margaret weighed in on that as well. She added, *"whether up at the hospital, at the school for the vigil, or finally at the memorial service, I watched as all the kids from all schools consoled each other. You saw rivals schools like Colonial Forge, Mountain View, Stafford, and Brooke Point, and suddenly the competition of sports took a back shelf. These boys and girls knew Justin and were grieving too. They were amazing, because within each other's comfort, they all served as equal support for one another. I have worked in the education field for thirty five years, and I have never seen one single thing or cause, consume an entire school, and community as everyone rallied around Justin."* Margaret paused for a couple minutes, and I knew that she was welling up in pain as she remembered something at that very moment. She softly said, *"I had a talk with Justin one day, and I remember how he looked up at me and said that "nothing matters to me. What about my parents and Jordie?" That is how Justin always was. He never put himself as the center of anyone's concern. He always worried about everyone else's pain, with little regard of all that he was going through."* Tom poignantly remarked, *"I remember sitting in our gym for Justin's memorial service, and I was thinking, where do we ever go from here? Justin's illness and eventual passing lasted for close to two long years, yet from our perspective as teachers, I think it also helped us all better understand the needs of each and every student. We started to do 'lists of school concerns,' along with our ever present personal thoughts and prayers. We felt the surge of an entire school and community, as everyone ran hard for Justin at every turn."*

There was little doubt that our talk on this day, would at some point, center on Courtney. Both Margaret and Tom said that how she pulled herself through this entire ordeal, was truly nothing short of spectacular. Margaret said, *"she was taking AP courses, which were terribly challenging in itself. She was the class SCA President, all the while never skipping a beat in any of her work, and she was up at the crack of dawn training for softball. To this day, I honestly cannot understand how she did all that. When she received her beautiful promise ring from Justin, I was truly worried about her road ahead and what she was being promised. Yet, she stood tall despite the tremendous toll of pain within her heart. I think that is why she did not surprise me when she stood in front of everyone at the candlelight vigil and spoke. Wherever Courtney Crews had to be, she was there. I think her own personal demeanor, attitude, and spirit in general bolstered everyone."* Tom nodded his head with every one of Margaret's words and said, *"for a girl her age, to garner enough strength to go on day after day, was absolutely phenomenal. She did everything and more amidst circumstances that were so heartbreaking at times. I would look at her and wonder how she could possibly cover all the bases that she did, and never once did she break. She bent but never broke, which I think astounded everyone."*

We talked for a few minutes about the dinner and talent show at North Stafford, in support of Justin and his family. The later evening hours would see Justin don his cap and gown in a private ceremony. Tom immediately said, *"as I watched everyone helping out and readying for the dinner, show, and then making things special for Justin's graduation, I truly saw how* resilient, and giving people in general can be during times of need. Justin's tragic illness pulled an entire community together as one. It let me know how one life could impact so many. Everyone, including total strangers, came together for one cause. It served as a reminder to me that regardless of our likes and dislikes, we are all still compassionate, caring human beings. We are all on this planet for at least one reason…compassion for others. Now, if there is some way we can bottle it up, and never forget its true meaning to equal what we found in each other after Justin's death, that would truly be something very special."

Margaret commented that North Stafford was hosting the Commonwealth District Gymnastics Tournament earlier that day as well. Margaret said, *"the gymnastics team, and all of their helpers never stopped from early morning, until late into the night. As soon as the tournament ended that day, they rolled right into Justin's dinner and talent show. Everyone was bone tired, but you could just see on everyone's faces that there was something you had, and wanted to do, because they knew how Justin had been fighting."* Again, as Margaret told me that story, I could sense that she was becoming emotional as she brought that night back to her mind. She bowed her head slightly and added, *"the Valedictorian was on stage that night, and sat behind her baby grand piano. Her brother was to assist by playing the violin. I remember how she looked out at the crowd and said, "I don't know most of you, but I picked out a song with a good beat that should help to pick up your spirits." That to me painted a picture of the whole demeanor of everyone during this awful time. Everyone stopped what they were doing whenever an activity centered around Justin, and unselfishly chipped in. It seemed to be a way of life now."*

After talking about the dinner and talent show, our conversation centered on the special, private graduation ceremony Justin had in February of 2008. Tom and Margaret concurred that Justin took no shortcuts of any kind, and made it very clear that he valiantly earned every credit necessary to graduate. He was in tremendous pain, but Tom said at the end, *"Justin knew that he had met all the requirements. In some cases he went above and beyond the call, considering what he was going through physically, and emotionally."* Margaret remarked that after most had left the gym that night, Justin's closest inner circle remained for the proud ceremony. She said, *"he was in so much pain, and was so very weak that he could not really talk. But if you look closely at that glow in his smile in the cap and gown photo, you would* never even know he was sick. He was absolutely beaming." Tom spoke about something Justin said to him just before this ceremony, and 'why' it was so important to him. He said, "Mr. Nichols, I just want a picture at graduation for my dad and family, a picture taken while I can still stand, look normal, and be wearing my robe." Margaret took this opportunity to say to Justin, "I am not congratulating you now Justin, not here in February. I will wait until June when I see you walk across that stage with your classmates." Margaret said that Justin looked perplexed and said, "well what will I do then?" Margaret said, "you will walk across just like everyone else, and then I will congratulate you Justin. Justin just looked at me with that smile."

As our conversation started to wind down, I sought to ask Thomas and Margaret what their thoughts were then, and how the memory of Justin remains now, some five months after his passing. Margaret first spoke of something that she will never get out of her head, nor does she seek to wish it away. She solemnly said, "quite honestly, he had warmth within his smile, and when he looked at you and smiled, it naturally made you smile and feel good too. I hold a vision of him always smiling at me, while forever wearing his baseball hat. You could never guess in a million years how sick he was. Justin Whitaker never took the stance that it was ever all about him. He always empathized with others. He had courage beyond courage and never gave up. I had a very close friend who had cancer, Debby Ryan, from UVA. She always said you "never give up...never." That was Justin's voice too. He never stopped fighting. Even if doctors wanted to test a new drug, or try radical means to treat him that were extremely painful, he would say, "let's have at it." So many times I saw what he was enduring and said to myself, most adults could never deal with so much pain and so many disappointments, but not Justin. Even when he was sick, could barely walk or talk, he would come to North Stafford events, and try to stay for as long as he could. If he was in pain he never said a word. He just slipped away into the night after saying goodbye. If I were to use two words to describe him, it would be courage and perseverance. Those were the true cornerstones of Justin. I don't think I will ever lose the memory I have of him smiling at me as he wore his baseball hat...never."

Tom softly added, "I truly believe that God did pick him out as our little Superman, to unite us all together. He had unparalleled courage, and a will to fight, in ways that I had never seen in a young teenager. Courtney was the mirror image

ON THE SEVENTH DAY OF APRIL....SUPERMAN DIED

of Justin in that way. They both showed their peers the importance of life, and living each moment to the fullest. I do think God used Justin as his Superman here on Earth. It was so difficult for all of us to watch as Justin slipped away. The sorrow, and the impact on all the kids and within the community, was devastating. I think each of us viewed death in a far different way afterwards. I am left with an emptiness that I am sure most can relate to. He was a special young man, with a special message for all of us. His legacy will live on, and I do believe we have all been taught that everything we learned from Justin's death, is for a far greater cause."

While visiting Craig's house one evening, I became privy to yet another act of kindness that did not emanate from any one person. It came in the form of the Senate of Virginia, Joint Resolution No. 5023, 'Celebrating the life of Justin L. Whitaker. The Resolution was supported by Patrons-Stuart; Delegates: Cole and Howell, W.J. Shortly after his death, on April 23, 2008, this Resolution was agreed to by both the Senate, and the House of Delegates. Throughout the Resolution, it basically ran the course of Justin's life, from birth to death, with the most memorable stops in between. It spoke of family, baseball, Mickey Mantle, his love for Courtney, his cherished North Stafford High School, and for his gutsy, determined "never give up" creed. In closing the Resolution stated;

WHEREAS, Justin Whitaker will be greatly missed by his loving family, his numerous friends and admirers, and the residents of Stafford County; now, therefore, be it

RESOLVED by the Senate, the House of Delegates concurring, That the General Assembly mourn the passing of an outstanding young Virginian, Justin L. Whitaker; and, be it

RESOLVED FURTHER That the Clerk of the Senate prepare a copy of this resolution for presentation to the family of Justin L. Whitaker as an expression of the General Assembly's respect for his memory.

Craig and I privately talked later, and said, *"to this day, all of our families tried to figure out who made this resolution possible, and we never knew who may have such political power to honor Justin in such a way. Someone clearly held a great grasp on all that was Justin from the beginning of his life, winding through everything he did, and all the people he loved along the way. This gesture by the Senate and the State of Virginia, absolutely floored all of us. It was just another reminder of how much Justin touched everyone's lives, in some form or fashion."*

The Spiritual World of Justin Whitaker

In one of our family meetings to make the ever so tough choices of deciding on what pictures to place within the book, I had the privilege to meet Wilma Garraway, from Stafford, VA. Wilma was clearly a guiding religious, spiritual force in the lives of the Whitaker children when the boys were young, and at the latter stages of Justin's life. Wilma said, *"I met Justin when he was about six years old when he first came into our church with his brother Jordie, and his mom, Shelia. My son Benjamin played baseball with him, and they soon became friends. When I had the occasion to pray with Justin, it was very special as I watched his strength dealing with this horrible cancer."* Wilma herself was a cancer survivor, and felt bonded to Justin in many spiritual ways.

On one occasion, Wilma spoke of an occasion when she, Shelia, Justin, and Jordie were in the basement and decided to have a prayer session. Wilma explained that, *"there was something demonic near Justin that night, and all of us heard this odd, soft laughing sound. There was no computer on, and our prayers continued and the laughing and presence seemed to disappear."* Wilma said that Zac showed up a short time later, and Justin excitedly told him about the occurrence, and how they made whatever evil spirit that was there vanish. Jordie would later speak about several occasions when he was home in Justin's presence, and all alone in the house, especially in the basement, when confronted by what he called, *"good and evil visits."*

Wilma's brother from Myrtle Beach, S.C., directed her to a Pastor in the area, who also served in a church in Washington, D.C. Wilma commented that, *"Pastor Frank never even knew Justin, and he thought that it was important enough to visit him at Children's Hospital. Justin was at his treatment for close to three hours, but on that day, Pastor Frank said he had a very prophetic message sent to him by the Lord for Justin. This was amazing. This Pastor knew nothing about Justin, yet told him that the Lord told him to "take a baseball* to Justin." The Pastor knew nothing about Justin's love of baseball, nor anything else that Justin had accomplished in his life. To this day though, I can still see Justin smiling from ear to ear. Justin knew that God had sent Pastor Frank to him."

As we were about to finish, Wilma said, *"Justin absolutely loved the Lord. He had a special, unique relationship with Him. I can clearly remember Justin saying was, "you know me Wilma. You know what and how I feel." All I could say in response was to tell Justin that the Lord had taken his hand and has lead him all the way. I believe Justin got his incredible strength and fight to live from the Lord. From the time his mother raised Justin in church, and taught him of the lessons of God, I believe it affected him in ways that truly paid off when stricken with such a horrific disease. Unless someone has been in his shoes fighting this fight, they cannot possibly understand what Justin endured. His greatest concern was always the same…hoping that his family would be o.k. He loved them more than life itself, and even in the worst of times, he tried to do the very best he could for everyone. I always joked with Justin and told him that I felt like his second mother. He knew in his heart and soul, that I would never say anything to him that I would not say to my own son. I loved him dearly, and I know I will see him again someday."*

Jordie Whitaker had yet another set of eerie tales to share regarding Justin's spiritual side, yet it came in the form of visitors he had never expected to meet. When Justin was first admitted into the hospital in 2006, Jordie said that he and Justin were alone in the room for a while. Jordie said, *"I glanced toward the window in the room, and I saw some type of demon-type figure crouching down, and elevated in the upper corner of the ceiling. It did not look like a person at all, it was more ghostly looking, and he appeared to be very dark in color. I didn't see it there long, and after that, I never mentioned it to Justin until about two weeks later. The odd thing was though, my Aunt Dee Dee came in the room about thirty seconds after it disappeared. I never said a word to her and she paused and said, "is everything alright in here Jordie. I just felt the darkest presence."*

Things remained very calm for about a month, until something else surrounding Justin happened that was equally stirring. Jordie said that this time, he and Justin were home. Jordie said, *"I walked into Justin's room, checked on him and said goodnight. I woke in the middle of the night and saw that Justin's door was slightly cracked open. I glanced inside and saw this brief flash of light that was golden-white in color. The light was coming somewhere directly above*

ON THE SEVENTH DAY OF APRIL....SUPERMAN DIED

Justin's bed. I looked up and something slowly materialized into what looked to me like an eighteen year old boy. Justin was sound asleep, and I looked at this boy and asked, why are you here? He never answered, so I asked, is there anything you can say? Can you hear me? Finally, after several seconds, the boy softly said, "yes." He said very slowly and quietly, "I was sent here to look out for things. I am the guardian watchdog tonight. My name is Mark." I asked Mark what happened to you, and he said, "I passed away from cancer five years ago." He didn't say anything else, and at one point during the silence I said, is it o.k. if I go to bed? He said, "Go, I'll be watching over you too." The strangest part of Mark's visit was, in the morning when Justin woke up, he told me that a "real young guy named Mark came to visit me last night." I could not believe he said that and also mentioned Mark's name."

Jordie explained that the nighttime visits had not reached their finale. He said, *"about one month after Mark's visit, it was close to two in the morning when I woke up in the house. I saw what looked like a blurred object on the side of the wall. Then at the upper corner of my room, I saw these two small red dots, like eyes looking down on me. There were no words spoken, but then I saw movement and Mark showed up to my right. The demon-like figure didn't move and said nothing. I did hear a soft grunting noise and a muffled laugh though. When I looked back at Mark, I saw what looked to be like eagle feathers on his back, and he was holding a staff in one of his hands. I turned and said, Mark why are you here? He said, "Justin prayed before he went to bed tonight, so I am here guarding over everyone in the family." I looked in the direction of the two red lights and told the demon he was not welcome here, but he just made those same odd noises. I think though, he knew he was not welcome, because it seemed to be enough to make him drift away. It was really odd when he left too, because as soon as his presence left the room, I felt this amazing heaviness leave with him. Mark moved away from me toward Justin's room and said, "I will be in the other room if you need me."*

In the summer of 2007, Jordie was entertained by yet another visitor. Jordie recalled that, *"I was alone in the basement doing my usual, playing video games with my headset on. All the lights were off and like the flash in Justin's room that night, I see a quick flash out of the corner of my left eye. I didn't pay attention to it right away, until it happened the second time. All of a sudden, there was a young girl of about eight years of age walking around the corner slowly toward me. My first impression was how much she looked like Lisa Linares, Justin's friend from Inova Fairfax Hospital. Since I had that encounter with Mark, I felt calm...not scared.*

I asked how she was and what happened to her? She said, "me and my mom were driving down the road when a drunk driver hit us. I was in the back seat and was only six years old at the time." I asked her why she was here, and she said, "I am not here to guard you. I'm only here now to make you happy. If you ever need help, you don't have to pray, just call my name…Johanna." She stayed near me for about ten minutes, then moved to where she came from and disappeared."

Jordie said the summer passed, and in the fall of 2007, he was in his usual entertainment location, the basement, playing video games. Jordie said, "I had my headset on, but in the background I could hear a different noise. I heard what sounded like the soft beating noises of a drum. Once again as before, there was a very brief flash of light, and I turned and saw what I believed was about a twelve year old boy walking to me. He had an old, Civil War type drum hung around his neck, and he was holding two wooden drumsticks. I said hello and tried to engage in conversation with him for several minutes, but he said nothing. He then said, "I'm here to comfort you like Johanna did." Then he walked toward the end of the couch and sat down. But, it was really weird because it was like we were existing in two different atmospheres. He sat there for about ten to fifteen minutes and then said that he knew how he had died. He quietly said, "I never died from anything in the war. I had tuberculosis. It ran in my family." He then appeared to get very sad but then said, "I can't really cry in front of you." After a minute or so, he just stood up, and walked away."

To top the whole spiritual theme off, Craig mentioned something else that may have had Justin's name all over it. We all know of Justin's precocious, funny ways. Right after his funeral, everyone started to gather at Craig's house to relax and unwind after a long, hard few days…months. Many of the flower arrangements and items from Justin's memorial had been placed out on the deck to make room inside the house. Craig said, "it was a gorgeous afternoon, probably 70 or 75 degrees out. Justin's friend, Justine Bushore, decided to sit outside and it was still outside with a very slight breeze. Justine sat down and was overcome with grief as she looked at some of the arrangements surrounding her. All of a sudden out of nowhere, a gust of wind kicked up, and one of the arrangements blew over and landed in Justine's lap. It was a heart-shaped flower arrangement, with the number seven in the middle. There was no explanation how it landed right in her lap as she was crying in sadness. I believe it was Justin's way to say, don't cry for me anymore. I'm o.k. now. As for

ON THE SEVENTH DAY OF APRIL...SUPERMAN DIED

Justine, she was a little shaken up and went inside. Humorously a few minutes later though, I remember how she said, "there you go. That's just like Justin for you!" Justin lifted her spirit for her."

As Jordie finished his stories, he said, *"after Justin passed away, I have never seen any spirits since, and you can almost feel this calmness now inside the house...odd."* Shelia Whitaker later added, *"to be quite honest with you, I almost believe that Jordie witnessed a spiritual battle waged between good and evil as Justin's body weakened and his condition worsened. There is no explanation for it other than that."* Quite honestly, as I listened to Jordie recount those mystical, spiritual visits over the time span of Justin's illness, I was left with the surety that he *did* see and feel something. This was not the imaginative mind of a young boy seeking attention. He remembered the occasions with clarity as to when they occurred, and what words were spoken. To be quite honest with you, I was left a little bit spooked as I walked up the dark street toward my truck later. I was hoping someone was watching over me.

Final Memories of Justin "Playing the Game"

There were sides of Craig Whitaker that I came to know years ago, when serving as a Stafford baseball coach, on into AAU. Whenever, and wherever you saw Craig, you saw Justin and Jordie nearby. I learned through Craig that since his divorce, when the kids were five and six years old, he had his life was consumed as a full-time dad. Craig said, *"even though times were hectic and crazy, juggling a full-time job, and making sure their needs were met, I would not have given up one moment. We were big Baltimore Oriole fans, and tried to get to Camden Yards as much as we could. It was fitting that with Justin's illness, he was able to meet the greatest Oriole of all time, Cal Ripken. Cal was absolutely amazing with our family. One time when Justin was too sick to go to Baltimore, Cal signed over twenty items for me, Courtney, Jordie, and Zac. Cal surprised Justin though, by calling him from his cell and talking to him for about twenty minutes. It made Justin's day. Cal and Mickey were Justin's two baseball icons. Cal Ripken was as gracious up close and personal, as he was between the lines playing baseball. I can remember when we went to O's games when Justin was young, he would always say that "someday dad, I will be wearing number seven and patrolling the outfield for the Orioles...someday." He never got that chance. Following Justin's death, we made a trip to the Hall of Fame dinner and were allowed to mingle with all the greats because of Justin's induction. I saw Cal behind us, but he was eating dinner and I didn't want to bother him. When he was through I walked up and told him that Justin had died. An expression of sadness was on his face in seconds, and he extended the most heartfelt condolences to us. He was a true class act and made a huge impact upon Justin's life."*

Craig talked about Justin and Jordie playing in the Stafford Baseball League, but Justin also played AAU baseball which basically travelled every weekend for tournaments once the season kicked in. Some of the road trips traversed the eastern seaboard, and Craig recalled that, *"it was often very late when we returned on some Sundays for AAU tournaments. Jordie would be asleep on the back seat, but Justin always stayed awake and was my trusty*

ON THE SEVENTH DAY OF APRIL....SUPERMAN DIED

co-pilot. We would have talks about everything, but it always seemed to return to baseball subjects. Even then, as a young boy, he knew it was late and didn't want me falling asleep. I think back now at how big his heart was then and it still hurts. That was just Justin. When I think about his death now, I still think baseball, because so many players from old AAU squads, and other high school teams were at his memorial service to honor him. I told people that Justin always made sure I was safe driving, and now it was my turn to make sure that he found his way home the right way. I now know 'why' Justin stayed up late driving with me. He protected me and I him. That is why I wanted to be sure he found his way safely home in heaven."

In a related baseball theme, Craig spoke of Geraldine Day, the wife of deceased Negro League Baseball Hall of Famer Leon Day. Leon was elected into the Baseball Hall of Fame in 1995. Craig wanted to honor Geraldine in many ways for as he said, *"Geraldine became a very special friend of our family. I first met her at a baseball show in 1996. That started a friendship and a bond that remains to this day, and will last a lifetime. In 1998, the boys and I were invited with Ms. Day to join her for the induction ceremonies as special guests of hers. It became an annual time of joy for all of us. Justin and Jordie were eight, and nine years old at the time. Because we were with Ms. Day, we were able to meet all of the Hall of Famers being inducted, as well as those that returned every year for new ceremonies. Justin and Jordie felt so special to be surrounded by such greatness. They cherished all of the autographs from so many tremendous Hall of Famers. When Justin was twelve, his AAU baseball team, the Virginia Thunder, travelled to Cooperstown to compete in a nationwide AAU tournament of 64 teams, while staying, and playing on the beautiful fields there. Justin always talked about the fantastic week there and said, "it was the best time of his life."*

When Craig reflected on that trip to Cooperstown, I was honored to be one of the coaches of that very solid, Virginia Thunder squad. Russ 'Rusty' Berry was the head coach, and Mike Loving was another assistant coach with me. The picture of that Thunder team lies within this book, because as I look at Justin's face, and that of my son Nick, along with all of those fine boys…Al, Cody, Jimmy, Jake, Jason, Sammy, Blake…all, it truly becomes emotional. I watched each and every one of them grow into fine young athletes, and the men that they are today. When we see each other, even now, it is with a hug, and not a handshake in our greeting. Their faces on our Thunder team remain emblazoned within my mind, because it was a time in my life that I will cherish. That single snapshot carries not, the truest meanings of the past as we sought to enjoy time with, and guide these fine young men. That is why when Justin died, all of these ballplayers were back in their Thunder uniforms, and became twelve years old again. We shared these emotions because we had lost one of our players in Justin, and all we have left are the lasting memories of time shared on a baseball diamond.

I told Craig, Shelia, and everyone who loved Justin that I remember him best as an integral player on that Virginia Thunder baseball team. You see Justin's eyes sitting in the front row of that team picture, and you felt his presence and desire to be the best he could be. He never got the chance to fulfill his dreams, finish his high school baseball play, and move on into college. Yet in his presence, he helps us now to move on and realize 'why' the great game of baseball made each of us happier...stronger. Justin was 100% correct. It was the *"best of times"*...the very best.

Justin's red Cooperstown jersey from that 2002 Cooperstown trip, with of course his cherished number seven on the back, was on display for his memorial. Numerous players mentioned above from the Thunder team, wrote messages on Justin's shirt, of how they felt, now six years later as they honored a teammate no longer with them. Jason Kittell wrote, *"Superman...we're all thinking about you at Colonial Forge. Every time I take the field, you will be the one I think of. I'll play for you, pray for you, and live through you for the rest of my life. Love you kid, Jason."* Colin McManus penned, *"I enjoyed every minute we spent together, and know you will be with me every time I'm on the mound. Every pitch is for you. Love, Colin."* I think the last note hit me the hardest because it was my son Nick's writing. I stood in Justin's bedroom and noticed the Cooperstown shirt on a hangar behind the door now. It was one of those take your breath away moments...difficult to describe. I know and love all those boys, but seeing your own child's name there, made it seem all the more painful that Justin had left us. Nick wrote, *"Hey man. You're in my thoughts and in my prayers. You will always be my Superman and always in my heart. Love you, Nick."* The words seen scrawled upon a baseball shirt memorialized a player that I can assure you, will never be forgotten. The Virginia Thunder coaches and players, along with anyone else who ever took the field with Justin Whitaker anywhere, would have said the same things. We lost one of ours. You will make our journeys through life full and complete, simply because you have shown us the way to honor each day as if it *were* our last. Your spirit and fight lives on Superman, and all of us are thankful for each and every moment shared with you. God speed Justin Lee Whitaker.

One Year's Passing

We all understand how calendar pages callously flip from one month to another, and there is amazement as time flies by in our busy lives. To me though, it absolutely floored me that it was now April 7, 2009. One year had passed since Justin's death and it seemed so surreal to me. The sun desperately tried to peek through the cloud cover on a very brisk, windy day in Stafford County, Virginia.

Early in the morning I sent text messages to Craig, Shelia, Courtney, and Zac. I wanted them to know that I understood that their hearts may have been very heavy. For Zac especially, I also had great difficulty imagining how hard it must have been to awaken on April 7th. He held full realization that his best friend had been gone one year, and that the date of Justin's death coincided with his own birthday. There was an odd sense of irony for Zac. It was hard to believe Justin had been gone a year, and it fell on the same day when family and friends sought to celebrate another birthday with him. Over time I have come to understand *why* Zac was such a special young man. He was the mirror image of his best friend in life, Justin Whitaker. To see him now as he moves on in life, serves as an eternal honor to Justin's memory.

I also sent a message to Courtney in the early morning hours of April 7th, and felt it best to let her quietly contemplate this year's passage of time. I made plans to meet everyone at the cemetery later that afternoon. At close to 3:30 p.m., I walked to the gravesite alone, staring down at Justin's final place of rest. I was happy that I had a few moments to myself as I shared my thoughts and prayers with him. At the gravesite, there were many beautiful flower arrangements left by some who chose to honor his memory in anonymity. Shelia had made a beautiful arrangement that she had placed at the base of the site. It was shaped like a large baseball, with the number seven prominently centered. I stared down to see images of Justin on his gravestone as well. He was a young boy, a twelve year old

ON THE SEVENTH DAY OF APRIL...SUPERMAN DIED

athlete at the Hall of Fame games, a proud graduate, and a smiling, powerful Superman. All of Justin's moments in life were captured forever as I paused in quiet contemplation of this fine young man.

Shelia arrived at the cemetery first, closely followed by Craig and his parents, Barbara, and Darrell Whitaker. Jordie arrived next with Amber. We all hugged and shared warm words on this very chilly, spring day. Darrell told me that there were plans for a family get together soon in Michigan. We laughed about how cold it was there and I questioned why the reunion was not done in a warmer locale. I glanced over to the left of the gravesite to see Amber drop to her knees and share tears on this solemn day. The gravity of this occasion honoring Justin's passing was clearly too much too handle. As Amber rose and stepped away, we hugged and I understood the pains she held inside. It truly was unfathomable that a year had passed since Justin's death. Simply standing at his gravesite and the images before you, brought everything back into clear focus. We all knew Justin was in a far better place, but missing him was always a constant.

As we were preparing to leave, Craig had asked me if I had heard about the article in that week's Stafford County Sun newspaper. He told me that Jim Lawrence had done a story relating to Justin's one year anniversary, but that there was an even bigger surprise. In 2008 when I interviewed North Stafford High School principal Tom Nichols, and Athletic Director Margaret Lowry, they told me their plan was to have Justin's name on a new scoreboard at the baseball field, along with a memorial stone placed near home plate. Craig and Shelia said that another dedication was to take place honoring Justin yet again. The Stafford County School Board, in a unanimous vote, agreed to rename the Wolverine's baseball complex, the *Justin Whitaker Memorial Baseball Stadium*. The dedication date chosen was June 10, 2009, three days before Justin's brother Jordie was to graduate from North Stafford.

Akin to the movie *'Field of Dreams,'* somehow you felt that on that special night in June, Justin would mystically emerge through the fencing. Proudly wearing his NSHS baseball uniform, sporting his beloved number seven, Justin would trot onto the fresh, cut grass and take his place in center field. The public address announcer would tell all in attendance, that this field he loved so much would forever be named after him. Justin would turn to the crowd, tip his cap, and sporting his wry smile, nod to all who honored him. He then assumed a fielder's position, slightly crouched, and readied his glove as if a game had just begun. Justin returned to his cherished North Stafford baseball diamond one last time for all of us. His legacy had reached its pinnacle, and we are forever blessed by all that he left behind. With a gentle wave of his hand to the crowd, Justin jogged back toward the centerfield fence, and disappeared into the night. For all of us he left behind the finest of memories…and in his own sweet words…*the very best of times.*

Hey brother,
Everybody misses you. I wish you could still be here with us, but I'll never call you back here again to suffer.
Love Ya Brother,

Jordan Whitaker

TO THOSE I LOVE AND THOSE WHO LOVE ME

When I am gone, release me, let me go,
I have so many things to see and do,
Please don't tie yourself to me with tears,
Be thankful for our beautiful years.
I gave you my love. You can only guess
How much you gave to me in happiness...
I thank you for the love you each have shown,
But now it's time I traveled on alone.
So grieve a while for me, if grieve you must, Then let your grief
be comforted by trust.
It's only for a time that we must part,
So bless the memories within your heart.
I won't be far away, for life goes on.
So, If you need me, call and I will come.
Though you can't see or touch me, I'll be near.
And if you listen with your heart, you'll hear
All my love around you soft and clear,
Then, when you must come this way alone,
I'll greet you with a smile, and say "Welcome Home! "

Written by:
Therese Marie Horn